McGRAW HILL FINANCIAL | McGRAW-HILL EDUCATION

ONE PROUD LEGACY, TWO POWERFUL COMPANIES

125 YEARS OF ESSENTIAL INTELLIGENCE

New York   Chicago   San Francisco   Lisbon   London   Madrid   Mexico City
Milan   New Delhi   San Juan   Seoul   Singapore   Sydney   Toronto

1 2 3 4 5 6 7 8 9 0   DOW/DOW   1 8 7 6 5 4 3

ISBN: 978-0-07-180870-5
MHID: 0-07-180870-1

e-ISBN: 978-0-07-180871-2
e-MHID: 0-07-180871-X

TABLE OF CONTENTS

FOREWORD
BY HAROLD McGRAW III

As we set out to write the history of McGraw-Hill for our 125th anniversary, we faced a challenge: The story of our company could not end where the past ends because we continue to make history in the present. Only by connecting the past and present could we show how the values of innovation and integrity, instilled in our infancy, have endured even as markets and technologies have changed. Only by looking to future years could we explain the momentous decisions that we have made in recent months.

In September 2011, we announced plans to create two powerful new companies to bring greater focus to our two key businesses, education and financial information, which enjoy remarkable opportunities for innovation and growth. From one company, we will form two—McGraw Hill Financial and McGraw-Hill Education. The former will be a leader in analytics and benchmarks in the capital and commodity markets; the latter a leader in personalized digital learning. This decision, which was made following a year-long strategic review by management and the Board of Directors, ensures our employees can excel in two distinctive sectors and can continue to do what they have always done—give people the insight and intelligence they need to make decisions vital for their future.

Just over one year later, in November 2012, we announced an agreement to sell McGraw-Hill Education to Apollo Global Management. After carefully considering all of the options for creating shareholder value, our Board of Directors concluded that this agreement generates the best value and certainty for our shareholders and will most favorably position the world-class assets of McGraw-Hill Education and McGraw Hill Financial for long-term success.

The pages that follow tell the story of a company that has achieved its potential in every era by helping countries, markets and individuals achieve theirs.

During the Industrial Revolution, when entrepreneurs and workers needed to understand the new technologies reshaping America's economy, a former schoolteacher named James H. McGraw began publishing journals on topics from railways to electricity.

During the Great Depression, when the U.S. federal government demanded increased transparency from corporations, experts at what would become Standard & Poor's turned these filings and reports into analysis that investors could trust.

During the years after World War II, when America's universities welcomed a new generation of students, McGraw-Hill published seminal textbooks such as Paul Samuelson's *Economics* that made knowledge more accessible.

In the 1950s, when investors demanded faster ways of measuring the stock market, Standard & Poor's showed how a machine printing perforated paper could churn out an index that has become arguably the most influential in the world—the S&P 500.

The examples go on. Through oil spills and embargoes, Platts has brought transparency to commodity markets. Through economic booms and busts, people around the world have turned to the brands of McGraw-Hill for insight and trusted information. We hope that will never change.

Looking to the future, we see new trends giving rise to an economy that rewards intelligence and knowledge above all else. As globalization has narrowed the gap between developed and emerging markets, digitization has connected people around the world like never before. With data crossing oceans at the speed of a keystroke, a race for insights and intelligence has begun. Having two companies will better position our brands to help customers develop the two forms of capital needed to win that race—financial capital and human capital.

For McGraw Hill Financial, the focus will be on helping countries and companies develop the capital and commodity markets needed to create jobs, improve infrastructure, confront demographic challenges and grow a stronger and more secure middle class. We are excited by the bright prospects of McGraw Hill Financial. From Standard & Poor's to Platts, the company's premier brands are best in class and sit in the heart of attractive, growing markets. In a world awash with more data than anyone can understand, our credit ratings, indices and other benchmarks stand apart as indicators that markets can trust.

For McGraw-Hill Education, the focus will be, as it always has been, on helping societies and individuals develop the human capital needed to fill today's jobs and spur tomorrow's innovations. The digitization of education offers the opportunity of the century to personalize learning around the needs of students anywhere, anytime. With a history of pioneering new pedagogy, we are once again pushing the frontiers of education.

I am optimistic about McGraw-Hill's future because I have seen over and again how we have successfully met challenges of the past. The common thread has always been the character and innovations of our employees. They were our greatest strength 125 years ago, and they remain our greatest strength today. I cannot thank them enough.

Ultimately this book is not the story of a company. It is the story of the men and women who made a company—the visionaries, the innovators and the strivers. The tradition that began during the Industrial Revolution continues today in the global knowledge economy, and I am honored to be part of it. From one inspiring legacy, we go forward as two powerful companies.

Harold McGraw III
Chairman, President and CEO
The McGraw-Hill Companies
November 27, 2012

McGRAW HILL FINANCIAL
ESSENTIAL INTELLIGENCE

VISION

McGraw Hill Financial is a high-growth, high-margin benchmarks, content and analytics company in the global capital and commodities markets.

MISSION

We are driven by promoting sustainable growth by bringing transparency and independent insights to the global capital and commodity markets.

VALUES

We are committed to the highest standards of fairness, transparency and impartiality with our customers, partners and colleagues. We are committed to the highest standards of integrity and honesty in all our dealings.

McGRAW-HILL EDUCATION
WHERE THE WORLD LEARNS TO SUCCEED

VISION

McGraw-Hill Education is a digital adaptive education technology leader whose highly-personalized learning experiences prepare students of all ages to succeed.

MISSION

For over 100 years, we have been helping people use knowledge to succeed. We are committed to providing students, teachers and professionals with the latest technology.

VALUES

We are global, partnering with students, educators, and other professionals worldwide to offer the best products. We are committed to developing technology to improve learning.

McGRAW HILL FINANCIAL | McGRAW-HILL EDUCATION

ONE PROUD LEGACY, TWO POWERFUL COMPANIES

125 YEARS OF ESSENTIAL INTELLIGENCE

1

ONE PROUD LEGACY, TWO POWERFUL COMPANIES

Every successful company continuously reinvents itself to create new products and services as the world and customer needs change. The hallmark of McGraw-Hill's success has always been to invest in intelligence and insights, from the emerging railroad technologies of the 1880s to the global capital and commodities markets of today. The culture of McGraw-Hill has always been dedicated to customer service and innovation and the ingenuity of its employees and their ability to adapt has helped McGraw-Hill thrive far longer than the half-century most multinational corporations survive.

The outlook can be seen through the lens of two separate companies. In 2012, McGraw-Hill announced it would create McGraw Hill Financial and McGraw-Hill Education through the sale of the education business to Apollo Global Management. Establishing two strong independent companies was part of a broader strategy, announced a year earlier, to accelerate growth and enhance value for shareholders. By creating McGraw Hill Financial and McGraw-Hill Education, McGraw-Hill CEO Harold McGraw III said at the time, "Our Growth and Value Plan will transform a multifaceted corporation into two powerful companies, each with highly focused strategies, aligned customer bases and interconnected markets."

Both companies benefit from well-known, powerful brands and enduring trends in expanding markets.

McGraw Hill Financial boasts a stable of some of the most iconic brands in finance and business. Those brands are: Standard & Poor's, S&P Capital IQ, S&P Dow Jones Indices, Platts, J.D. Power and Associates, McGraw-Hill Construction, and Aviation Week. The combination of global brand recognition and scale gives McGraw Hill Financial unmatched opportunity both to expand its leadership positions in existing markets and to enter new growth markets. These well-known brands power a leader in the global capital and commodities markets that in 2012 generated about 40 percent of revenue (and growing) from outside the U.S. This high-growth enterprise offers clients insights, research, and analytics, including credit ratings, indices, portfolio risk analysis, price assessments across commodities markets, equities and fixed income analytics. These offerings are essential to customers and are deeply embedded in their business processes and workflows. McGraw will lead the company as Chairman, President and CEO.

In divesting McGraw-Hill Education and positioning the new McGraw Hill Financial for faster growth, Chief Financial Officer Jack Callahan said, "The proceeds [from the sale] afford us even further financial flexibility. We already had a very strong balance sheet and this transaction gives us greater opportunities to make investments and return cash to shareholders."

He added, "2012 turned out to be a remarkable year for McGraw-Hill. The businesses that will make up the new McGraw Hill Financial delivered a great performance and our teams around the world did extraordinary work to standup two terrific industry-leading businesses."

As an independent company, McGraw-Hill Education, a name known to generations of students, will be headed by Lloyd G. "Buzz" Waterhouse, a former IBM executive who led another educational publisher before being named company CEO in 2012. The company is a leader in instructional design, digital learning, customized content and educational service that helps improve student and professional performance.

Few things are certain about the future, but for McGraw Hill Financial and McGraw-Hill Education, there are at least two assurances: global expansion and digital innovation offer significant opportunities for long-term growth.

Consider this: In 2012, emerging economies were expected to account for 80% of world economic growth, up from about 47% five years earlier. Going forward these economies will need to develop their financial markets to channel domestic and foreign savings more efficiently into productive investment, according to researchers at the International Monetary Fund and Brookings Institution.

Or this: The world population is expected to add 2 billion citizens, a 27% increase, between the end of 2011 and 2050. Meanwhile, the number of people age 65 and up will double globally, to 1 billion, from 2012 to 2030. The spending and savings implications for governments, businesses, investors and individuals who will care for an increasing number of citizens are profound.

Another development to think about: There were an estimated 6 billion mobile device subscriptions in use worldwide in 2012 and that number will overtake the world's population by 2015. As technology improves, wireless networks expand and consumers increasingly move to mobile devices of all kinds, the need for trusted digital content is expected to grow, too.

All of these trends underscore one point: Powerful global shifts are creating exciting opportunities for McGraw Hill Financial and McGraw-Hill Education to help investors, governments, businesses, and students achieve sustainable economic growth and success.

As the world grows, higher-powered economies like China and India play an increasingly important part in the global community. To achieve their long-term growth potentials these countries must meet rising demand for new roads, schools, highways, airports and energy.

Increasingly, the global capital markets are being turned to in order to fund these projects. A huge amount of debt will need to be refinanced and new funds will need to be raised in the coming years. Standard & Poor's estimates that bank loan and debt capital markets in the world's biggest economies will need to finance more than $40 trillion of corporate borrowing between 2012 and the end of 2016. The Asian Development Bank estimates that Asia needs to spend $8 trillion between 2010 and 2020 to meet the region's basic infrastructure needs.

This enormous need is expected to accelerate the growth and emergence of local debt markets around the world as alternative funding sources to banks, which continued in 2012 to deleverage from the 2008-09 financial crisis. This provides significant opportunities for Standard & Poor's to rate an expanding number of bonds.

The number of older persons has tripled over the last 50 years and will more than triple again over the next 50 years, according to the United Nations. How can an aging population spur demand for the insights of McGraw Hill Financial? The tens of millions of citizens 60 or older in countries like Brazil, China, India, Indonesia and the United

States, increases the need for independent, objective research, analytics and benchmarks from S&P Capital IQ and S&P Dow Jones Indices to help inform the decision-making of pension fund managers and other professional investors. These professionals will be focused on overseeing the assets needed to fund the retirements of a growing number of clients.

In financial markets awash with more and more data, and volatility, investment professionals will need sophisticated investment research and analytics platforms. Enter S&P Capital IQ, which helps a growing client base identify investment opportunities, draw unique insights and increase returns.

Greater consumption of raw materials like steel to build the infrastructure of tomorrow coupled with the rise of commodities as an asset class also spell greater opportunities for McGraw Hill Financial. Platts is guiding the way. Platts is known around the world as a leading source of price assessments in the physical and financial commodities markets. For many commodities, Platts' price assessments are considered benchmarks for establishing prices in contracts and monitoring risk. The expansion of Platts in the steel market offers a window into its growth potential. As industries have moved from long-term contracts to short-term spot market pricing, the $2 trillion steel market benefits from Platts' price assessments for iron ore, metallurgical coal, ferrous scrap, and other commodities that span the steel market. Miners, steel producers and other customers look to Platts for more than 850 price points for steel and related raw materials. It is clear that as commodities markets evolve there is a growing premium on the transparency, benchmarks and insights Platts offers.

The trends in the global education market are no less powerful than those in financial markets. Take, for instance, that students everywhere are demanding the smarter use of technology. They expect learning to be delivered when they want it, where they want it, and how they want it.

The proliferation of smartphones, tablets and other mobile devices offers an intriguing opportunity. Ponder what a World Bank study in 2012 had to say: "Mobiles are arguably the most ubiquitous modern technology: In some developing countries, more people have access to a mobile phone than to a bank account, electricity, or even clean water. Mobile communications now offer major opportunities to advance human development," including offering access to education.

To meet the needs of health care professionals around

1. S&P's Infrastructure Views blog features reports and commentary from S&P analysts on topics such as transportation and renewable energy technologies. 2. S&P Capital IQ offers financial professionals powerful research and analytics to enable them to find key opportunities and success. 3. Treasures is a research-based Reading Language Arts program for grades K-6. 4. Students and teachers collaborate online through the CINCH Learning system for math and science.

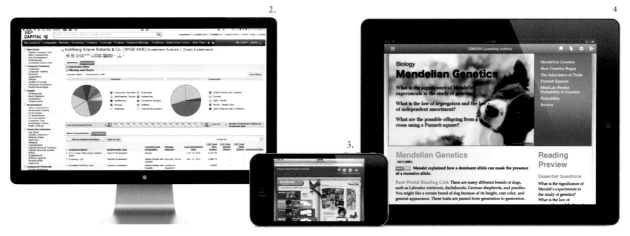

1. 2. 3. 4

the world, McGraw-Hill Education's digital Access platform enables universities, libraries and research institutions in more than 65 countries to subscribe to its trusted content from leading scientific, technical and medical titles. In Nigeria, for instance, McGraw-Hill's online medical products are available to all higher education institutions.

For the U.S. high school market, McGraw-Hill in 2012 began offering interactive math and science programs specifically designed for Apple's popular iPad.

Waterhouse said: "My lifetime commitment to learning and to technology convinces me that it's time to accelerate the transformation to digital education so that students, teachers and administrators can reach their real potential and improve learning for individuals everywhere in the world."

While McGraw-Hill Education races ahead to support learning across a growing number of digital devices, the company continues to deliver on the fundamental promise that educational opportunities open the doors to a better life. Governments around the world know that education is the key to sustainable economic progress. The need for skilled, educated workers to fill the jobs of today and tomorrow will continue to drive McGraw-Hill Education for many years to come.

Yet, too often students entering the workforce, from India to Indiana, lack the skills required by employers. In fact, 34% of employers worldwide experienced difficulties filling vacancies due to lack of available talent, according to a 2012 survey by the Manpower Group. The consulting firm McKinsey projects a shortfall of 1 billion educated workers by 2020.

McGraw-Hill Education is helping to fill this knowledge gap. In places like India the company sees a growing need for vocational-skills and English-language training to fill jobs and it is meeting this need with innovative programs. McGraw-Hill Education is supporting students with the introduction of professional development certification programs in India focused on the retail and banking industries. By combining real-world instruction, on-the-job training, and job placement assistance, participants are "job ready" upon completion.

In China, where the demand for skills development is large and growing, McGraw-Hill Education uses a joint venture started in 2011 to equip students ages 5 to 14 with 21st century skills in creative thinking, collaboration and teambuilding, which are necessary for success in college and in the workforce.

McGraw-Hill's own workforce has been the backbone of the company's success and its employees will continue to propel

1.

2.

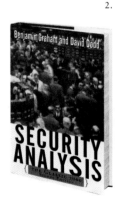

3.

4.

McGraw Hill Financial and McGraw-Hill Education forward.

"We have great businesses in exciting markets," said John Berisford, executive vice president, Human Resources. "But that's just a small part of the story. It is the talented and committed men and women of McGraw Hill Financial and McGraw-Hill Education that set us apart, and it is their ingenuity and commitment to excellence that give me great hope about the future of both companies."

Ted Smyth, executive vice president, Corporate Affairs, is excited by the growth opportunities ahead. "None of our competitors can offer the level of essential intelligence that McGraw Hill Financial can, across credit ratings, indices, equity and fixed income analytics, commodities information and research," he said.

While the McGraw-Hill name is now linked to separate companies, the missions remain the same.

"Both companies share a common promise. And they both share a common purpose. We're about helping customers find ways to succeed and to prosper in a rapidly changing world, where information is often conflicting, confounding, and confusing. The bottom line is that we help make sense of it all," McGraw said.

"To be clear, our mission is never—nor never will be—about us. It will always be about our customers and their markets. We're committed to helping our customers succeed in the knowledge economy that knows no borders and where everyone can prosper and reach their fullest potential."

Above:
McGraw-Hill CEO Harold McGraw III and Roopa Kudva, CEO of India's leading ratings agency, CRISIL, celebrate the opening of the company's new headquarters in Mumbai in 2010.

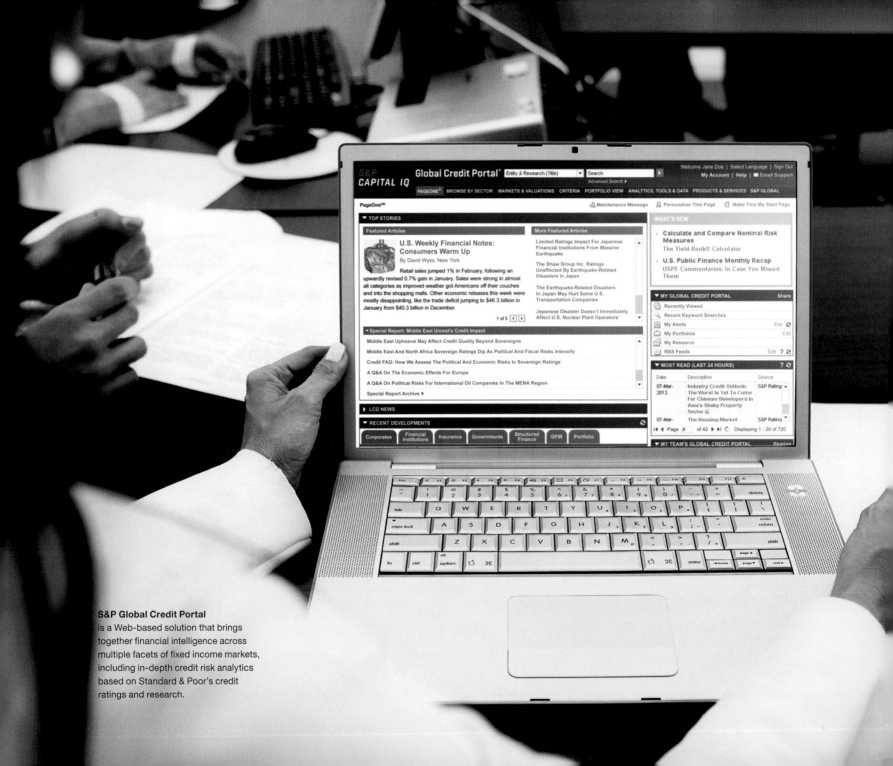

S&P Global Credit Portal
is a Web-based solution that brings together financial intelligence across multiple facets of fixed income markets, including in-depth credit risk analytics based on Standard & Poor's credit ratings and research.

2

CREDIT RATINGS: A KEY TO ECONOMIC OPPORTUNITY

"Capital goes where it's wanted and stays where it's well treated," observed former Citicorp chairman Walter Wriston. But what enables the flow of that capital? The answer is trustworthy information, such as the credit ratings and research of Standard & Poor's.

Ratings play a vital role in global financial markets by reducing "information asymmetry" or the knowledge gap between borrowers who issue debt to finance any number of projects or operations and the lenders or investors who can provide that funding. Because a borrower knows its own creditworthiness better than a lender does, ratings serve as an independent, unbiased "second opinion" the lender can use to gauge whether it will be paid back on time and in full. The overall result should be a superior allocation of limited capital to productive uses.

Take, for example, the African nation of Ghana, which launched a $750 million international bond in 2007 to help finance critical infrastructure projects such as roads and power plants. S&P's credit rating on that bond helped Ghana communicate to the world the relative cred-

it quality of the debt and provided a pool of global investors an independent benchmark to evaluate the creditworthiness of Ghana's bond.

Chile wasn't even planning on issuing bonds when it requested a rating from S&P in 1992. It just wanted to demonstrate that its credit standing had recovered from the Latin American financial crisis of the 1980s. Chile saw the sovereign rating as a benchmark that could enhance the private sector's access to capital markets and help attract foreign direct investment.

In the world of corporate bonds, ratings help companies to access capital markets to fund expansion projects or operations, which can in turn establish new technologies. For instance, FPL Energy National Wind received a rating by Standard & Poor's on $365 million senior notes in July 2011. The company is repaying its debt to investors with revenue generated by converting wind energy into electricity and selling it to utilities and others. The rating spelled out weaknesses and strengths in the business—all of which is extremely useful to investors weighing

their decisions. The rating explained that the company is seeing high costs and its output is beholden to something it can't control—the amount of wind. But it also said that National Wind's projects are diversified because it uses four different wind turbine technologies and reserves are in place to support the company's liquidity.

Over the years, through periods of economic growth and contraction, ratings have endured because they help bring clarity by creating a common language to assess and compare risk. By 2012, S&P, which McGraw-Hill acquired in 1966, had 1,400 analysts in 23 countries to help inform decision making.

Offering the market informed opinions has propelled S&P from its first rating made by its forebear, Poor's Publishing in 1916, to the 1 million-plus credit ratings it published as of 2012.

S&P's progress is made possible by the company's independent process of forming ratings. Because S&P analysts "call it like they see it," their opinions about credit risk are sometimes subject to criticism. In the late 2000s, economic uncertainty swept the globe as many countries in Europe experienced crises of international confidence due to their high national debt. Numerous European countries, including France, Austria, Italy, Portugal, Spain and Belgium, were downgraded by ratings agencies. S&P had anticipated the debt crisis by lowering the ratings on sovereigns such as Greece and Portugal several years before the market confidence crisis in the eurozone began to intensify in 2009.

Subsequent downgrades, S&P said, were primarily driven by analysts' assessments that the policy initiatives that have been taken by European countries may be insufficient to fully address ongoing systemic stresses in the eurozone, including tightening credit conditions, simultaneous attempts to de-lever by governments and households, and weakening economic growth prospects.

Some European observers claimed the rating agencies had "Western bias" and that the downgrades accelerated the eurozone's spurious debt crisis.

But expressing such decisions—criticized or not—is S&P's

core function. The company's role is to provide an independent opinion of creditworthiness that is globally consistent. S&P's views are based on a common set of public criteria. These criteria comprise a range of quantitative and qualitative factors, including S&P's view of key economic and political risks. That's why the majority of its employees are local nationals outside the U.S.

"Local knowledge is critical. That's why analytical decisions are made predominantly by people in the local market or region," McGraw-Hill CEO Harold McGraw III said.

In August 2011, S&P cut its sovereign credit rating on the United States. The move was prompted by S&P's view on the rising public debt burden in the U.S. and its perception of greater policymaking uncertainty, consistent with its published sovereign rating criteria. The move was met with criticism from some in the U.S. government. But S&P stood firm on its ratings, assumption and criteria—all of which are transparent, so investors can make their own determinations about an issuer.

Since 1975, an average of 98.9% of investment-grade sovereigns have not defaulted on their foreign currency debt within 15 years, compared with 70.3% of those in the non-investment grade category. And an International Monetary Fund study of sovereign ratings concluded they had a strong track record. No rated sovereign has ever defaulted within a year of being rated investment grade.

The need for an independent agency to offer informed, objective ratings of the debt-worthiness of issuers was apparent nearly a hundred years ago. Two ancestors of Standard & Poor's—Poor's Publishing and Standard Statistics—each began rating corporate bonds and municipal securities, respectively, in the early 1920s, and by 1927 they started assigning ratings to foreign governments that issued debt in the United States. By 1941 the newly merged Standard & Poor's was publishing a Bond Guide with lists of corporate and municipal bond ratings.

In the late 1960's scores of corporate borrowers increasingly relied on short-term, unsecured loans raised in the marketplace—called "commercial paper"—as opposed to borrowing from commercial banks. This largely unregulated market had grown from $4.5 billion in 1960 to nearly $40 billion by mid-1970. Commercial paper borrowers had traditionally been the highest quality companies in the U.S. and the investors were usually other corporations with excess liquidity to invest for short periods of time. There was one company that assigned ratings to commercial paper (and its ratings were

subsequently deemed unreliable) so there was little insight into the state of these investments.

One of the commercial paper market's largest borrowers was Penn Central Transportation Company, parent of the Penn Central Railroad. Formed by the merger of the Pennsylvania Railroad and the New York Central Railroad, the company wasn't able to integrate the two operations and began facing extreme liquidity problems in 1970. By that May, it filed for bankruptcy.

The bankruptcy— the largest in U.S. history at that time—was a shock and severely disrupted the markets. Many companies found it impossible to roll over or repay their commercial paper and turned instead to banks.

As a result, S&P, which began to rate commercial paper about a year before the bankruptcy, but not Penn Central, was swamped with requests for its commercial paper ratings. S&P's commercial paper ratings became the industry standard and that single event catapulted S&P to the essential role that it plays in the financial markets.

In the mid-1970s, S&P virtually announced the coming of the financial crisis in New York City by suspending its bonds' A rating. The move made the public aware of the municipality's financial deterioration.

City officials were incensed but S&P held its ground. It said New York City's cash flow was inadequate, and its dependence on massive borrowing to pay for operating expenses was too great. Reports showed a $1.5 billion deficit. President Gerald Ford initially refused federal assistance—"Ford to City: Drop Dead," read the *Daily News'* famous headline. But a bailout, monitoring by the State and budget cuts helped improve the city's situation. Then-Mayor Abe Beame announced he would have to lay off thousands of workers and raise subway and bus fares. He and other city officials remained unhappy, but S&P insisted that its role was to be independent and keep investors informed.

"We decided that the situation had reached a point where default on a note issue or a failure to make a bond interest payment could be more real than imagined," observed then-S&P President Brenton Harries.

It was about this time, the mid-1970s, that one of S&P's most accomplished leaders started rising through the ranks. Leo O'Neill started at S&P as an equity analyst in 1968 and by 1975 was appointed vice president, corporate finance and chairman of the Corporate Bond Rating Board. In 1989 he was leading the firm's ratings business and in 1999, O'Neill was named president of the company, which at that time included equity research, credit ratings and indices. It was under O'Neill's guidance that S&P became the first rating agency to publish its ratings criteria and the first to launch a global network of offices to support the international growth of capital markets. During his tenure, Standard & Poor's substantially increased the coverage and global reach of its equity research capabilities, index business, and data coverage of companies. O'Neill also led Standard & Poor's efforts to recover from the September 11, 2001, terrorist attacks, which occurred only blocks from its downtown New York City headquarters.

In perhaps no other period of the 150 year-plus-history of Standard & Poor's has the capital markets been more volatile

and Standard & Poor's role more visible and scrutinized than in the late 2000s. In 2008, the U.S. economy was in trouble and citizens, lawmakers and the business community searched for answers. Some observers claimed one reason for the worst financial crisis since the Great Depression was that ratings agencies did not foresee that national housing market prices would collapse by 35 percent. The fact is very few anticipated such a collapse, including the U.S. Federal Reserve and global economists.

"The current crisis has demonstrated that neither bank regulators, nor anyone else, can consistently and accurately forecast whether, for example, subprime mortgages will turn toxic, or to what degree, or whether a particular tranche of a collateralized debt obligation will default, or even if the financial system as a whole will seize up. A large fraction of such difficult forecasts will invariably be proved wrong," Alan Greenspan, who served as Chairman of the Federal Reserve from 1987 to 2006, explained in 2010.

The extent of the decline in the U.S. housing market,

On Left:
Standard Statistics, precursor to S&P, moves to larger accommodations at 345 Hudson Street in New York City in 1930.
Above From Left:
Leo O'Neill, who became president of S&P in 1999, helped propel S&P to become the world's benchmark provider of ratings and other data. **CreditMatters** helps professionals keep up with S&P's global perspective on credit markets.

Traders in the 30-year bond options pit at the CME Group in Chicago.

the worst since the Great Depression, caused S&P to downgrade some AAA rated subprime-mortgage-backed financial instruments and some eventually defaulted. The company's ratings of U.S. mortgage-backed securities in the 2005-2007 period clearly did not match S&P's strong historical track record. S&P's ratings were based on assumptions about the U.S. housing and mortgage markets which factored in declines, but not as steep as the ones eventually experienced.

S&P's then-President Deven Sharma testified about S&P's role in the market before congressional committees. Of the residential mortgage-backed securities, he said in 2009 that: "S&P is profoundly disappointed with the performance of many of its ratings. Although we always expect that some portion of the debt we rate, even highly-rated debt, will ultimately default, our ratings of mortgage-backed securities issued in this time period have been unusually unstable and their performance has not matched our historical track record."

He said the assumptions about the assets were from a robust analysis of the transactions, market monitoring and S&P's years of experience rating these types of securities.

Learning from the experience, S&P was the first rating agency to announce a broad set of new actions to reinforce the quality and independence of its ratings process and better serve global capital markets. Among the actions: increase staff training, compliance and quality reviews of credit ratings, enhance the criteria used to rate securities and independent reviews and approvals of the criteria and models used to rate issues and issuers. Between 2009 and 2012, McGraw-Hill invested more than $200 million in systems, training and analytics to enhance the quality of S&P's ratings.

As a result, S&P emerged from the crisis a stronger organization with enhanced processes and procedures to provide the market with opinions based on thorough, independent analysis. There is also added regulatory oversight of rating agencies to assure investors that the agencies are meeting these standards.

"Standard & Poor's is one of the largest and most respected financial research organizations in the world. Given the importance of ratings in the capital markets and the historic times, I can't imagine a more exciting mission and vantage point," said Paul Sheard, who was named S&P's Chief Global Economist and Head of Global Economics and Research in June 2012.

"Ultimately, our success depends on the value our ratings provide to investors in the market," said Douglas Peterson, who was named president of Standard & Poor's in 2011.

There can be no doubt that S&P's track record in corporate, structured finance and country ratings is strong. For example, the 5-year cumulative default rate for structured finance issues rated AAA has been 3.0%. The translation: Over time, the higher the Standard & Poor's rating, the fewer defaults.

"We have a world-class organization," said Peterson. "The commitment, integrity and talents of our employees set us apart. Having worked around the world in the financial services industry for more than 25 years I came to admire the work of S&P long before I joined the company. I am privileged to lead this team and extremely proud of the insights we provide."

Market trends are certainly favorable. S&P estimates that about $5 trillion in corporate debt will mature from 2013 through 2015. This large pool of maturing debt will need to be rated, and companies such as S&P will be there to provide issuers and investors with trusted research and benchmarks.

Peterson added that S&P's prospects will grow even brighter as local bond markets emerge and become more sophisticated. In addition, the trend toward capital markets—especially debt capital markets—bearing the burden of financing, rather than banks, will create more business too. That's because banks are being required to hold more capital and can therefore lend less. Still, bank loan rating will be a big factor in future lending too.

"The demand for credit from countries and companies to finance infrastructure projects and support growth are producing new and expanding bond markets from Tel Aviv to Johannesburg and throughout East Asia," he said. "S&P is committed to helping develop capital markets around the world. With our credit benchmarks and research across industries and asset classes and the local knowledge we have in these markets we play an essential role in fostering economic development and growth around the world. That gives me great optimism about the future."

3
PUTTING FINANCE UNDER A MICROSCOPE

Railroads were the biggest enterprises of their time. Astute businessmen such as Henry Varnum Poor and James H. McGraw knew that the most technologically advanced machinery also represented a tremendous opportunity to meet a market need.

For Poor, the rise of railroads instilled in him a sense that the public of the 1850s was entitled to know more about what went on behind the closed corporate doors of these companies that ranked among the biggest in the world. (Just a few decades later McGraw, a former schoolteacher from the village of Panama in western New York State, joined the staff of The American Railway Publishing Co. Read more about McGraw-Hill's founder in Chapter 20.)

More than a century after Poor's insights and desire for transparency, S&P Capital IQ employs the same principles in the financial intelligence and analytics it offers clients worldwide today.

"Independence and objectivity give our equity analysts the courage to make buy, sell, and hold recommendations," said Sam Stovall, chief equity strategist for S&P Capital IQ.

Information wasn't always so readily available. Poor felt that American companies were too secretive with their data.

"The only way to introduce honesty into the management of rail-roads is to expose everything in or about it to the public gaze," Poor wrote in 1857.

Eventually, Poor's company and its successors figured out a way to create a business out of serving the needs of their investor-clients by selling investment research that would help these clients make sound business decisions.

The task of collecting information set by S&P's forebears became easier after 1935, when the U.S. federal government began requiring many corporations to make annual, public reports on their finances to the Securities and Exchange Commission. S&P began collecting these and amassed a vast library of information, including newspaper and magazine articles, wire-service copy, Commerce Department publications, trade journals, and more. S&P analysts examined all this material, publishing their own analysis. By 1960, S&P was issuing more than 30 daily, weekly, and monthly publications. Four years later, it entered the computer age with Compustat, a database of global financial, statistical and market information.

By the 2000s technology, globalization, increasing amounts of data and the rise of new asset classes were fueling greater demand for valuable financial insights—exactly what S&P Capital IQ provides.

1. The S&P Capital IQ platform is used by investment professionals worldwide. 2. *The Manual of Railroads* is first published in 1868 by Henry Varnum Poor and his son. 3. Wall Street 4. 25 Broadway in New York City was an early home to the ratings business. 5. The Charging Bull statue on Wall Street is considered a symbol for the markets—aggressive and full of optimism and prosperity.

In 2004, Standard & Poor's acquired Capital IQ, a leading provider of information solutions to the global investment and financial services communities. In response to the rapidly changing and challenging needs of its global financial clients, the company created S&P Capital IQ in 2010, bringing together many of the key research, analytic and strategic capabilities of Standard & Poor's with Capital IQ's accurate and timely financial information.

During the period that S&P Capital IQ was formed, the markets were expanding rapidly and the appetite for financing was increasing. The global financial system reached $255.9 trillion in 2011, marking a 6 percent compound annual growth rate (CAGR) since 2008. And global market equity capitalization hit $52.9 trillion at the end of September 2012, with 12.6% CAGR from 2008 to the end of 2011.

As markets expand and become more complex, there are more opportunities for S&P Capital IQ's integrated data and analytics to inform clients' decision making. The company's products serve clients via desktops, data feeds and through on-demand and customizable delivery tools, so clients can see what they want, how they want it. The company's 7,000 employees in 20 countries provide on-the-ground access to every economy, market and region around the globe.

The business is a portfolio of capabilities that offers new and innovative solutions to the marketplace. The S&P Capital IQ platform provides financial coverage of 92,000 companies with more than 5,000 unique financial data items, global coverage of mergers and acquisitions, global market data, corporate earnings estimates and more. It brings together fundamental data, market-driven measures, and unique research to support efficient credit and market risk-driven analysis, with offerings that include credit ratings and research from Standard & Poor's, credit model scores from S&P Capital IQ, and gives retail wealth managers and financial advisors access to news and market intelligence to better serve their clients.

S&P Capital IQ equity research is well-respected in the financial world. Its analysts bring the highest standards of integrity, objectivity and rigor to their work. It had six winners in the *Wall Street Journal's* 2012 "Best on the Street" analysts survey.

S&P Capital IQ has responded to market needs through targeted investments. In April 2012, the company acquired Quan-

1.

2.

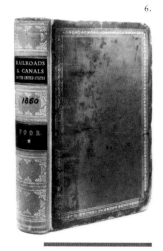

tHouse, which helps S&P Capital IQ provide its clients with access to exchange pricing globally, including securities valuations and portfolio analytics. Earlier in 2012, the company acquired R2 Financial Technologies, a provider of advanced risk and scenario-based analytics to traders, portfolio and risk managers for pricing, hedging and capital management across asset classes. And in 2010, the company took over the research and estimates business of TheMarkets.com, enabling S&P Capital IQ to offer buy side clients the most comprehensive global research and earnings estimates alongside the company's already best-in-class financial data and analytics.

Opportunities abound, according to Lou Eccleston, President, S&P Capital IQ and Chairman of the Board of S&P Dow Jones Indices. (In 2012, McGraw-Hill launched a joint venture combining S&P Indices and Dow Jones Indexes to create S&P Dow Jones Indices, the world's largest provider of financial market indices. See Chapter 4 for more.)

"We're facing change—systemic, regulatory, political and fundamental. But all this change generates opportunity. Over the past several years, we've accomplished much in a very consistent way. We've been able to look at changes in our markets and the 'gaps' that are not being filled by our competitors. We then have been able to scale our infrastructure and take to market integrated solutions through integrated delivery vehicles that fill market gaps," Eccleston said.

6. *History of the Railroads & Canals of the United States* by Henry Varnum Poor
7. Henry Varnum Poor.

NASDAQ CELEBRATES

S & P 500

50TH ANNIVERSARY

50 YEARS S&P 500

NASDAQ

Pick a "W

NASDAQ marks the
50th anniversary of
the S&P 500 in 2007
in New York City's
Times Square.

4
A COMPUTER LEADS
A STOCK MARKET
REVOLUTION

Observers routinely referred to it as "the electronic brain."

Actually, it was a Burroughs Datatron computer, located at the Boston lab of a company called Melpar Inc., then part of Westinghouse. The year was 1957. In went a perforated paper tape; its code contained the last hour's stock market data. Then with the press of a button, the giant machine began whirring—banks of lights flashing on desk-size consoles, multiple spools of tape spinning. Then, out popped the revolutionary S&P 500 stock index.

News reports were overwhelmingly positive about the index's creation. "Market Measured in a Flash," exclaimed *BusinessWeek*. "The stock market is in for the most comprehensive yardstick for measuring its ups and downs yet devised," proclaimed the United Press.

The S&P 500 was the brainchild of S&P's Paul Babson and Lewis Schellbach. Babson, chairman of the S&P Board, had heard that electronics-research company Melpar claimed the ability to produce indices of massive numbers of stocks electronically within a matter of seconds. He was sure that something could be made of this capability, and turned to jack-of-all-trades Schellbach to figure out what that should be.

A onetime *New York Morning World* reporter who'd learned the essentials of finance in the S&P trenches, Schellbach and colleague George Olsen spent a year refining the concept of the new index. Rather than averaging all stocks, the duo and Melpar's team opted for a basket of stocks that they deemed most representative. Their final list included 425 industrials, 25 rail stocks, and 50 utilities. These large-caps accounted for over 90% of the total value of all common stocks on the New York Stock Exchange.

The index provided what every stockholder wants to know: How is the market doing? For a long time that was a difficult question to answer. Imagine if you had a few shares of stock. Some might go down, others up. They might not only be moving in different directions but also at different speeds. Perhaps the changes reflected how each company was performing. Or perhaps they reflected something else—like a broader move in the market.

One of the first market benchmarks was produced in 1896, the stock index of the Dow Jones Co. now known as the Dow Jones Industrial Average. It took into account the price of each component company's stock, 12 in all. The Dow Jones Industrial Average was disseminated in broad tape—to distinguish it from ticker tape—by teletype starting the following year, in 1897. Despite using broad tape, many people did—and still do— refer to it as 'the ticker.'

In 1923, Standard Statistics—a forebear of S&P Dow Jones Indicies—began developing stock market indices weighted to take account of companies' relative capitalization. The first of these looked at 233 companies and was tabulated weekly. In 1926, Standard created a 90-stock index tabulated daily. And with the "electronic brain" the 500-stock index could be computed on an hourly basis. Within five years, it was being re-tabulated every five minutes.

"The S&P 500 ushered in a new era in finance," McGraw-Hill CEO Harold McGraw III said upon celebrating the index's 50th anniversary in 2007. "The S&P 500 is one of the great success stories in the history of business and commerce, and it is an integral part of the success story that is U.S. capitalism, which has as its lifeblood transparency, analytical rigor, and integrity. The S&P 500 both embodies and promotes all of these virtues."

In 2012 the S&P 500 was the world's most followed stock market index with $1.45 trillion directly indexed to it.

But there's much more to the index business than the S&P 500. S&P has been serving a huge appetite for investable and benchmark indices through innovation, creating thousands of new indices that span asset classes, geographic markets and investment strategies.

Between 2007 and 2011 alone S&P created more than 500 indices to meet client demand.

Since 2006, one of its most eagerly watched products has been the monthly S&P/Case-Shiller Home Price Indices, which track changes in the value of residential real estate for major metropolitan areas in the U.S.

In July 2012, McGraw-Hill brought together the two greatest names in financial indices when it launched a joint venture combining S&P Indices and Dow Jones Indexes to create S&P Dow Jones Indices, the world's largest provider of financial market indices.

McGraw-Hill contributed its S&P Indices business, a leading provider of equity, commodity, real-estate, and strategy indices. CME Group contributed its Dow Jones Indexes busi-

1.

2.

A man reads printouts generated by stacks of punch cards in 1946.

> "The S&P 500 is one of the great success stories in the history of business and commerce, and it is an integral part of the success story that is U.S. capitalism, which has as its lifeblood transparency, analytical rigor, and integrity."
> —McGraw-Hill CEO Harold McGraw III

ness, recognized for its strength in equity, commodity, emerging market, target date, and dividend indices. The pairing broadened a successful partnership between McGraw-Hill and the CME Group that began three decades earlier with the joint creation of the S&P 500 Futures contract. (See sidebar.)

S&P Dow Jones Indices calculates over 830,000 indices, publishes benchmarks that provide the basis for approximately 600 exchange-traded funds (ETFs) globally with $387 billion in assets invested by mid-2012. The joint venture is home to the Dow Jones Industrial Average and S&P 500, S&P GSCI and the Dow Jones-UBS Commodity Index, and many others. S&P Dow Jones Indices targets growth through international and asset-class expansion, new product development, enhanced market data offerings and cross-selling opportunities.

"More assets are directly invested in products based upon our indices than any other index provider in the world, and that is the byproduct of our extraordinary leadership, adaptive platforms and distinctive product offerings," McGraw said of the venture.

Alexander Matturri, CEO of S&P Dow Jones Indices puts it this way:

"Through our independent and objective viewpoints and expanding relationships with our partners and clients, S&P Dow Jones Indices plays a crucial role in the continuous development and growth of the world's financial markets. The ideas and solutions that we generate foster liquidity and confidence in the capital markets and serve as a catalyst for the investment community, enhancing our clients' ability to make better and clearer decisions for the long-term benefit of their constituents and the market at large."

The company sees endless permutations of its benchmarks. "Our goal is to provide an index for every type of investment," concluded McGraw.

INSPIRATION FROM THE S&P 500

Over the years, the S&P 500 has become a financial instrument depended upon by many in the investing world. In 1982, the Chicago Mercantile Exchange introduced stock-index futures based on the S&P 500, a development that "changed the nature of the financial-services world," in the words of then-senior executive Ira Herenstein.

The Chicago Board Options Exchange followed with stock-index options on the S&P 100 and S&P 500. Institutional investors in particular used these instruments to hedge portfolios or to buy and sell the entire S&P 500. And in 1993 S&P was at the forefront of the phenomenal growth of exchange traded funds or ETFs, when the first SPDR (Standard & Poor's Depository Receipts), a basket of stocks designed to track the S&P 500 that are traded throughout the day, was launched. By 2012, ETFs had become some of the most actively traded securities worldwide.

5

PLATTS: SHINING A LIGHT AND BECOMING A BENCHMARK

It started as a newsletter to help the underdog in a burgeoning new industry—oil. More than 100 years later, Platts enables thousands of traders, risk managers, analysts, and industry leaders in more than 150 countries to make informed and up-to-the-minute trading and investment decisions within the energy, petrochemicals, metals, and agriculture industries.

The market for oil had been building since the 1850s, when a Canadian scientist patented a method for extracting "rock oil" and refining it into a quality lamp fuel, which he called kerosene. Within a few decades, demand for that product had made Cleveland magnate John D. Rockefeller into a very rich and powerful man. By 1879, Rockefeller's Standard Oil controlled 90% of America's refining capacity.

Warren Cumming Platt, a young journalist, became fascinated with the oil business while covering legal battles between industry pioneers in Cleveland.

In covering those court cases, Platt saw a need for information and decided to enlist on the side of the underdog—the small oil producers, refiners, and distributors. In 1909, at the age of 25, he began the monthly *National Petroleum News* (NPN.) His aim was to cover oil-industry news across the board, but with special attention paid to concerns of "Independent Oil Men." Platt and his NPN colleagues set about to promote transparency and pave the way for greater competition through increased information flow.

Ongoing oil discoveries across the United States—in California, Texas, New Mexico, and Oklahoma—meant a steady surge of new players entering the industry. And then along came the automobile, stimulating huge new demand for petroleum products even as electric power was dimming demand for kerosene. By 1920, there were 9.2 million cars on American roads, creating a sizable demand for gas and all the businesses that go with it.

Platt understood what could really help the industry would be a public record of oil prices, which varied greatly. An absence of public information allowed speculators to buy and resell at high rates. NPN helped stabilize prices and end speculation with a regular publication of crude-oil and refined-product prices from various locations.

By 1923, the new publication *Platts Oilgram Price Service* was reporting prices and market data daily. The two-page newsletter was printed and mailed from offices in Tulsa, Cleveland, Chicago, and New York for overnight delivery.

Platts Oilgram rose to global prominence in 1928, when the three world giants at the time—Standard Oil of New Jersey, Royal Dutch Shell, and Anglo-Persian Oil—based an oil transaction agreement on the U.S. Gulf Coast oil price as published in *Platts Oilgram*. This established Platts' published prices as benchmark quality for oil business contracts.

McGraw-Hill acquired Platts in 1953. The founder stayed on as consulting editor. The corporation assumed publication of *Platts Oilgram Price Service*, *Platts Oilgram News Service*, and *National Petroleum News*.

Under Halsey Peckworth, named editor-in-chief of *Oilgram Price Service* in 1958, Platts gained and consolidated the global reputation it has maintained to this day. In 1960, he introduced the Channel Port Index—a price index created for major petroleum products at English Channel ports. The Channel Port Index was replaced in 1966 with the European Bulk Rotterdam barge and cargo quotations.

As the 1960s gave way to the 1970s, oil traders were using Telex machines to communicate their transaction confirmations. Platts followed suit and began sending Telex-delivered reports called MarketScans to supplement its print newsletters.

In the 1980s, Platts launched several electronic news services, including Platts Global Alert, first made available via satellite transmission. European Power Alert provided real-time information on the Continent's natural-gas and electricity markets. By the 1990s, these services became accessible through such third parties as Bloomberg, Dow Jones, and Reuters.

Trusted price assessments are an essential component of what Platts offers. In the petroleum market, Platts uses a price assessment process called Market-on-Close. The MOC is a structured, highly transparent process in which bids, offers and transactions are communicated to Platts editors and published in real-time throughout the day until the market closes.

After market close, Platts editors examine the data gathered with respect to Platts' stated methodology and specification guidelines, and publish price assessments that reflect the end-of-day spot value.

Platts launched the MOC process in Asia in 1992, in Europe in 2002, and in North America in 2006. By 2012, it was used by Platts editors in Singapore, London, New York, and Houston in dozens of oil and oil-related markets worldwide, expanding its use to other commodities.

In 2007, the company introduced Platts Editorial Window

1.   2.   3.   4.

(eWindow), which facilitates the price discovery process by combining Platts' Market-on-Close price assessment methodology with state-of-the-art technology customized for Platts and licensed from the IntercontinentalExchange (ICE). With its at-a-glance, grid-like format, eWindow provides a clear view of all bids, offers and transaction data communicated to Platts editors during the MOC price assessment process. It also allows participants, at the click of a mouse, to directly submit and confirm deal information to Platts and the marketplace simultaneously.

In addition, the tool's compatibility with ICE technology allows eWindow users to execute trades through ICE without leaving the Platts MOC price assessment process and environment.

A century after its founding, Platts' innovations in price discovery and information delivery continue to provide solutions to pricing challenges and help build its reputation as a leading provider of energy price information.

In 2011, the company acquired Bentek Energy, LLC, an energy market analytics company. In the same year, it bought the Steel Business Briefing Group, a leading provider of news, pricing and analytics to the global steel market, augmenting its coverage in the metals sector.

In 2012, Platts expanded into the agricultural space by purchasing Kingsman SA—a privately-held, Switzerland-based provider of price information and analytics for the global sugar and biofuels markets.

These investments are benefiting the company and positioning it for future growth. In 2012, McGraw-Hill Chief Financial Officer Jack Callahan said he was particularly pleased with Bentek's performance. "We're seeing double-digit growth for that enterprise, and we're quite excited about what that's adding to the portfolio," he said.

By 2012, Platts was producing more than 12,000 price assessments, references, and indexes daily. The company has continued to strengthen its position as a global leader and has more than 15 offices on five continents, serving customers in more than 150 countries. As of late 2012, Platts was McGraw-Hill's most global business, with almost two-thirds of its revenue coming from outside the U.S.

3. In 2011, Platts acquired Bentek Energy, an energy market analytics company. **4.** News, pricing and analytics about the steel industry are another sector of Platts' expertise after it acquired Steel Business Briefing Group in 2011. **Above:** The plants to refine oil, such as this one in 1911, became major industrial complexes during the oil boom.

McGraw-Hill CEO Harold McGraw III with James D. Power III at an event marking the company's purchase of J.D. Power and Associates in 2005.

6

TUNING IN TO THE VOICE OF THE CUSTOMER

In the late 1960s, James David Power III—a former Ford Motor Co. financial analyst—started a business gathering customer satisfaction data and selling it to auto companies. One of his first clients was the California operation of a then all-but-unknown Japanese forklift maker. Power and the company's head of auto manufacturing hit it off immediately. The executive's name: Tatsuro Toyoda, the man who in time would become Toyota Motors CEO.

Power and Toyoda agreed that customer satisfaction matters more than anything else in marketing. Toyota became Power's biggest client for many years.

Historically, car buyers were motivated largely by considerations including styling, horsepower, and pizzazz. J.D. Power's focus on quality and customer satisfaction would help change that. According to *Automotive Industries* magazine, J.D. Power's Initial Quality Study and Consumer Reports' Frequency of Repair Records are the two most respected independent measures of auto quality. J.D. Power and Associates' data and research are used by most major automobile manufacturers to set benchmark standards.

Power's way of looking at markets hasn't always won immediate acceptance. American auto industry executives often reacted angrily to Power's message that manufacturers must emphasize quality, reliability and customer satisfaction. Gradually, though, Power began showing companies how vital customer feedback can be.

A key moment came in 1973, when Power surveyed Mazda owners about that carmaker's innovative rotary engines. The study uncovered a serious defect in the motor's housing seal that could require costly repairs. The finding prompted Ford Motor to abandon a potential deal for rights to use the engine design.

"The Mazda study gave us great credibility and showed we weren't spokesmen for the industry," Power reported. By the mid-

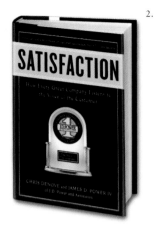

1980s, half of the company's revenues came from studies of the automobile business.

At first, Power performed proprietary studies for individual clients. But he found it worked better for everyone if he conducted independent surveys, the results of which were then offered to companies on a subscription basis. By the end of the 1980s, he was sending out four million questionnaires a year to vehicle owners worldwide.

The J.D. Power and Associates Initial Quality Study[SM] evaluates new-vehicle owners on their experience with problems encountered in the first 90 days after purchase, and the Customer Service Index (CSI) Study asks customers who have owned their vehicle for one year to rate their satisfaction with dealer service. High Initial Quality Study (IQS) and CSI ratings consistently correlate with higher customer loyalty and likelihood to recommend their vehicle and dealer. For this reason, they play an important role in many manufacturers' internal key performance indicators and compensation decisions.

Other automotive industry studies include Sales Satisfaction Index Study (which focuses on the initial sales experience), Automotive Performance, Execution and Layout Study (covering what consumers like about their new vehicle after 90 days of ownership), and the Vehicle Dependability Study (at three years of ownership). When the results are positive, carmakers often wish to report them in their advertising—which they are allowed to do after entering into a brand use licensing agreement.

J.D. Power and Associates became a unit of The McGraw-Hill Companies in 2005. In announcing the investment, McGraw-Hill CEO Harold McGraw III said J.D. Power and Associates was an excellent fit with The McGraw-Hill Companies.

"Both organizations share a long history and deep commitment to providing independent industry ratings and benchmarks that help businesses and consumers make effective decisions," he said.

In their 2006 book *Satisfaction: How Every Great Company Listens to the Voice of the Customer*, J.D. Power and Associates executives Chris Denove and James D. Power IV report that consumers are 50 percent more likely to spread information about a bad customer experience than loyal "advocates" are to talk about their positive

> ## "Both organizations share a long history and deep commitment to providing independent industry ratings and benchmarks that help businesses and consumers make effective decisions."
> ## —McGraw-Hill CEO Harold McGraw III

experiences. With the rise of social media, customers are making their own voices heard and giving feedback directly to companies. J.D. Power provides value to its clients in this realm by giving them strategic insight into these interactions through its social media research. Millions of unprompted consumer opinions gathered each year are aggregated and analyzed to provide valuable market intelligence about markets, trends, issues, brands, products and services, further extending the Voice of The Customer, for which the company is known worldwide.

The company has pushed beyond the automobile business into new industries, including telecommunications, energy and financial services. Some 40% of Power's revenue comes from outside the automotive industry. Customers and companies depend on J.D. Power and Associates rankings for everything from computers to credit cards, from mobile phones to hotels.

The company has expanded its global reach, too, and now conducts research in more than 50 countries. International markets include India, Japan, Taiwan, China, the Philippines, Indonesia, Thailand, Malaysia, Brazil, Canada, Mexico, United Kingdom, Australia and Germany. China is a major market for the company—and, indeed, J.D. Power is McGraw-Hill's largest business unit in that country.

With the continued expansion of China's domestic automotive industry, combined with J.D. Power's Power Information Network, proprietary research and automotive consulting work just a few short years after severe stress in the U.S. auto industry, J.D. Power was on track to record its best year ever in 2012.

An award given to companies that rank high in J.D. Power studies.

Dodge Global Network
is an online database
of more than 500,000
projects, with more than
5,000 updates daily.

7

INTELLIGENCE FOR THE CONSTRUCTION INDUSTRY

Sailing into New York harbor in 1904, expatriate novelist Henry James lamented the changes to the New York skyline.

"The multitudinous sky-scrapers standing up to view, from the water, [are] like extravagant pins in a cushion already overplanted," he wrote. Trinity Church, the tallest structure until 1890 thanks to its 284-foot steeple, was now lost among the tall buildings of lower Manhattan.

This was only the beginning. As America prospered, cities would spread out, populations grow, and the construction industry would become extremely important—and profitable.

Frederick W. Dodge recognized all this and started a business by providing information to construction companies and others involved in the industry.

In 1891, the young journalist began offering his specialized *Dodge Reports* in Boston, providing timely information about construction projects. Subscribers were allowed to specify the kind of information wanted—tailoring their reports by territory, project type and stage of construction.

Initially, Dodge got his information the old-fashioned way: He biked around Boston gathering leads on new construction. His first reports were simply snippets of information jotted down in longhand on slips of paper, which he then delivered the same way—on his trusty bicycle. Information had to be "early, dependable, detailed, and gathered from reliable sources by competent, trained employees," he decreed.

Dodge defined the project news service concept, collecting information from construction sources, processing it, and selling it to the major players within the industry who needed the intelligence to grow and succeed.

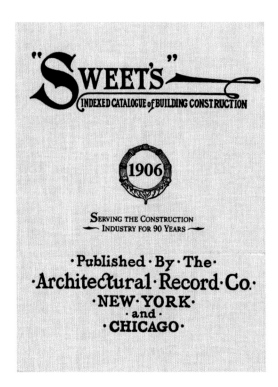

Left: *Sweet's,* shown in an issue from 1906, goes on to become the construction industry's most trusted source for building product information. **Upper Right:** A contract for Dodge to provide daily reports on construction in Boston in 1892. **Bottom Right:** Dodge MarketShare offers national reporting on construction projects and a customized solution with early-design, hard-to-find private construction projects.

Before long, he had a staff helping compose the reports, which were mimeographed from stencils composed in longhand. When a power mimeograph was invented that did the work of several hand printers, Dodge invested in the new technology.

A similar construction data service was being offered in New York by Clinton W. Sweet, publisher of the weekly *Real Estate Record and Builders Guide*, the *Daily Building Information Service*, and the high-toned quarterly *The Architectural Record*.

In 1896, the two competing outfits merged under the name F.W. Dodge Company. Soon after, *Dodge Reports* expanded to Philadelphia, Washington, Pittsburgh, and Chicago.

Dodge died in 1915, but his company continued to grow. By the late 1920s, it had departments devoted to coverage of construction news, construction-services catalogs, statistics and research. It also published magazines including *The American Contractor* and *Architectural Record*, which had evolved into a journal aimed strictly at a professional audience. *Dodge Reports* soon covered the 37 states east of the Rocky Mountains, with district offices in Atlanta, New Orleans, Dallas, Kansas City, St. Louis, Detroit, and Buffalo. The company also had acquired daily construction newspapers in Chicago, Denver, and San Francisco. Inexorable expansion followed, and by 1956 *Dodge Reports* had a presence in all of the then-48 states.

McGraw-Hill acquired Dodge in 1961. The corporation had long been involved in construction matters: In 1917, it merged two existing magazines to create *Engineering News-Record*, which became the leading publication devoted to civil engineering and construction.

Following the basic format carved out by F.W. Dodge, for decades *Dodge Reports* has served those at every level of construction, from architects to subcontractors, tracking projects from pre-planning through construction start. Each report lists the type, size, cost, and location of a project; its owner and architect; and the materials and services required along with deadlines for delivery. Gathering all this information is a considerable task: In 2012, Dodge relied on a pool of staff reporters located in more than 80 major metro areas who call on 35,000 sources each year, and cover 150,000 sources.

In 1989, Dodge began the move into the electronic age introducing Dodge DataLine, online access to *Dodge Reports*. In 2003, Dodge once again moved forward with The McGraw-Hill Construction Network (later named the Dodge Global Network), an online database of more than 500,000 projects, with more than 5,000 updates daily, and more than 65,000 digitized plans and specifications.

Dodge's digital transformation is leading the industry and its further commitment to business intelligence is unparalleled through services such as Dodge SpecShare®, Dodge BuildShare™, and Dodge MarketShare™. These services provide intuitive dashboards that take big data and translate it into actionable insight and intelligence—an industry first.

By 2012, *Architectural Record* had developed an extremely strong presence online and was the largest architectural website in terms of traffic—about 200,000 visitors each month. The community connects through photo galleries, where firms submit their own pictures of architecture around the world. There's also a strong community around continuing education, where some 1 million people have taken tests to maintain their credentials. In 2012, *Architectural Record* introduced the first continuing education unit (CEU) app, a free app that has received enthusiastic market adoption.

Engineering News-Record, too, has fully embraced the digital era. Its ENR News app has gained a robust following. ENR regional editions focus on local news. So, in addition to national coverage, readers can enjoy highly relevant local news.

Historically focused on the U.S. markets, McGraw-Hill Construction started to establish a more global footprint in 2012 by collecting international project data and making it available through its web-based Dodge Network.

In the same spirit as F.W. Dodge purchasing his first power mimeograph, McGraw-Hill Construction continues to invest in technology to create innovative offerings and serve its customers globally. As a result, McGraw-Hill Construction in the 21st century continues to lead the construction industry by gathering essential information and transforming it into actionable intelligence.

A group of men sit under Eugène Lefebvre's Wright Type A Flyer at Reims, France, during Aviation Week in 1909.

8

AVIATION WEEK: ESSENTIAL AT THE BEGINNING, LEADING TO THE FUTURE

From the biplanes of World War I, through the Jet Age and the Space Age, to modern aviation and aerospace technologies that enable global commerce and protect nations, the history of aviation has been, almost literally, the history of *Aviation Week*.

The original magazine—called *Aviation & Aeronautical Engineering*—was launched on August 1, 1916, just 13 years after the Wright Brothers' historic first flight. Its founder was Lester Gardner, who had worked at the *New York Times* at the turn of the century and would later serve in the U.S. Air Force during World War I and help found what is now the American Institute of Aeronautics and Astronautics. Gardner recognized the need for a technical journal of record that would serve as a clearinghouse for the great volume of technical data being amassed but not published.

With a degree in engineering administration from the Massachusetts Institute of Technology, Gardner was well positioned to produce such a journal. He had valuable connections in business, government, and the military and counted among his friends some of the best aeronautical minds in the country. Together with Augustus Roy Knabenshue—an American aeronautical engineer and balloonist—Gardner persuaded Orville Wright to rescue the flood-damaged Kitty Hawk airplane from storage in Dayton, Ohio, in order to put it on display at MIT, only weeks before the first publication of *Aviation & Aeronautical Engineering*.

Although the publication began with a technical focus, the industrial possibilities of flight were clear to Gardner in the wake of World War I. The war had stimulated advances in the structural strength of wings, bodies, control surfaces, and engine power. As flight evolved from a primarily military to a commercial orientation in the 1920s, *Aviation & Aeronautical Engineering* embraced a watchdog role.

At the end of that decade, the owners of the magazine—called, simply, *Aviation*—made a momentous decision. Riding the crest of the national financial boom in 1929, *Aviation* was experiencing the most prosperous period of its 13-year history and had doubled its staff. Selling

Space Shuttle
Columbia launches
in 1981, embarking
on America's first
shuttle mission.

the publication to McGraw-Hill Publishing could not have been an easy decision, but—coming as it did just eight months before the stock market crash that ushered in the Great Depression—it may well have spared *Aviation* the fate of other businesses that perished during the period.

Through World War II and the Cold War, *Aviation* played a critical role in covering what had gone from a hobby for wealthy enthusiasts to an essential industry. In 1960, to meet the increasing demand for knowledge created by the space race, McGraw-Hill merged *Aviation Week* with its sister publication *Space Technology*, to form *Aviation Week & Space Technology*, which added coverage of rocket design, moon landing efforts, and the politics of aerospace to its aviation reporting. The 1970s were a decade of transition for aerospace as an industry, giving way in the 1980s to the largest peacetime military buildup in U.S. history. The 1990s commenced with the first military conflict in the post-Cold War era.

Through the decades, the Aviation Week business has been there—not only reporting news but, also defining for the industry what issues and trends mattered and providing strategic analysis and insight to what has become a $2 trillion global aviation, aerospace, and defense industry.

The Aviation Week franchise is the industry's largest multimedia provider of news and information, serving customers in 185 countries. It operates 15 news bureaus worldwide, and its editorial team uses digital, mobile, and social media to engage with industry leaders and decision makers. Attendees of the Paris Air Show and the Farnborough Air Show —two of the top international aviation events—can make their way with Aviation Week apps that feature exhibitor listings, interactive maps, headlines, videos and blogs.

The relaunched *Aviation Week & Space Technology*, includes defense technology and Maintenance, Repair & Overhaul editions in a mobile-ready format with rich-media features. In 2012, Aviation Week made a strategic investment to add a 100,000-aircraft fleet database that extends its portfolio to defense, business aviation, and civil aftermarkets. Aviation Week produces leading industry events around the world that connect buyers, sellers and the global aerospace and defense community.

In sum, Aviation Week's integrated digital offerings deliver data, analysis, and forecasting tools that empower professionals in the aerospace and defense industries to conduct their business with a distinct advantage— more knowledge and expertise.

Shelton Fisher, president of McGraw-Hill Publications, which oversaw McGraw-Hill World News, watching the May Day parade in Moscow's Red Square in 1965.

McGraw-Hill World News Service, begun in the 1940s, grew into the world's largest newsgathering network devoted to covering business, industry, and technology.

By 1970 it had 11 U.S. bureaus with 55 correspondents and eight foreign bureaus with 24 correspondents and numerous stringers. Bureaus included London, Germany, France, the Soviet Union, China, Japan, Argentina, and Brazil.

McGraw-Hill World News reporters were charged with multiple responsibilities: to supply news to the company's many publications. They had to produce well-written, sophisticated stories that would appeal to the broad audience of

BusinessWeek. They had to report on developments in such areas as engineering and electronics for technical McGraw-Hill publications such as *Engineering News-Record* and *Electrical World.* And they were assigned tasks as diverse as helping to build McGraw-Hill magazine circulation, selling advertising, and developing authors and sales outlets for the company's book division. Some were even given market-research assignments for other corporations.

The Cold War proved a particular challenge. It was understood that News Service reporters were to cover trade matters, scientific breakthroughs, and even military

developments. One correspondent might attend a trade show in Moscow as another investigated a new hydroelectric dam in Colombia. Suspicious minds—such as those at police and intelligence services—tended to view such pursuits as troubling.

In 1948, Moscow bureau chief Robert Magidoff was expelled from the Soviet Union on charges of espionage, and two years later, three World News reporters were kicked out of Czechoslovakia. A photographer succeeded in getting shots of aircraft in the sky over the Moscow Air Show, only to have photos taken at that city's marketplace confiscated by the authorities. In Buenos Aires, correspondent John Wilhelm was summoned before the Argentine secret police and warned against Magidoff-like activities. Even in friendly London, McGraw-Hill faced charges over alleged violations of the state-secrets act.

In 1986, the restored Moscow bureau joined other World News bureaus in Europe to cover the Chernobyl nuclear disaster and its aftermath.

Some of the adventure and glamour of the News Service's salad days can still be recalled decades later. Describing his mid-'40s experience

in South America to a Columbia University historian in 1956, Wilhelm—who went on to become World News' editor-in-chief—told of a precarious flight over the Andes from Peru to Bolivia. Checking into the unprepossessing Sucre Palace Hotel in central La Paz, he found the hotel register required him to put down the name of his employer. "I wrote down the McGraw-Hill Publishing Co., and the clerk looked up with the most astonished look on his face and said, 'You are the fourth man from McGraw-Hill to check in this week.'…This greatly impressed the clerk and impressed me, too."

The News Service operated from 1945 to 1988, when the company dissolved the business, reassigning most correspondents to other publications. The News Service had operated as a way to inform McGraw-Hill's publications but by the late 1980s, the company decided those publications had very focused news demands and should be responsible for all of their own coverage.

"We're holding them responsible for the bottom line, so let's give them as much control as we possibly can," said Ralph Schulz, who was senior vice president for the company's editorial operations.

1.

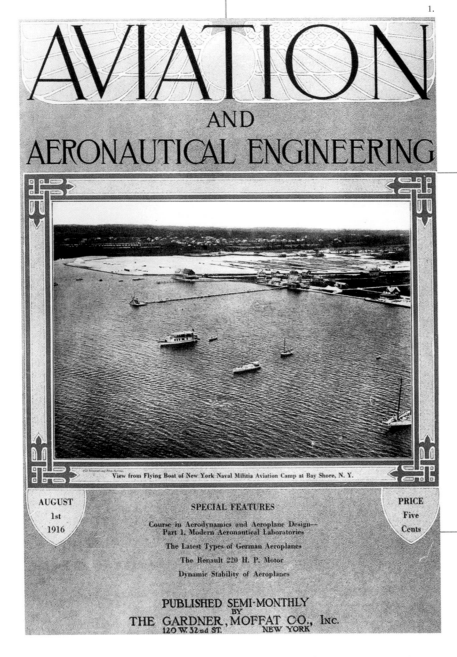

AVIATION
AND
AERONAUTICAL ENGINEERING

View from Flying Boat of New York Naval Militia Aviation Camp at Bay Shore, N. Y.

AUGUST 1st 1916

PRICE Five Cents

SPECIAL FEATURES

Course in Aerodynamics and Aeroplane Design—Part 1, Modern Aeronautical Laboratories

The Latest Types of German Aeroplanes

The Renault 220 H. P. Motor

Dynamic Stability of Aeroplanes

PUBLISHED SEMI-MONTHLY BY
THE GARDNER, MOFFAT CO., INC.
120 W. 32nd ST. NEW YORK

2.

1916-1919
THE PIONEERING OF AMERICAN AVIATION JOURNALISM
-AN IDEA IS BORN-

PAUL MANN

Luker D. Gardner

June 15, 1917

Aircraft manufacturers are now experiencing the same difficulties that in the past have confronted other great industries. An unprecedented demand has developed for aeronautical engineers. Unfortunately, there are but few fitted for the open positions. Engineers in other lines cannot qualify; their training and experience have run in different channels. Students in engineering schools, seeing no indication that aviation would be offering attractive inducements, have neglected the opportunity of specializing in the new science. There are practically no engineers available.

Aviation and Aeronautical Engineering
Nov. 10, 1916.

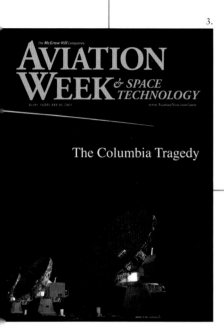

AVIATION WEEK & SPACE TECHNOLOGY

The Columbia Tragedy

3.

AVIATION WEEK & SPACE TECHNOLOGY

RELAUNCHED!

Aviation Week & Space Technology is powered by the cerebral energy of the deepest-digging, best-connected and most experienced team of journalists in the industry. **Relaunched July 2** with an even greater focus on technology, and **expanded** coverage that now includes defense technology and MRO editions. Also, the new *AW&ST* digital edition is mobile-ready on all platforms with much more interactive content. *AW&ST* has never been more powerful and essential to your information and communication needs.

To learn more about the new *AW&ST*, please visit
www.AviationWeek.com/newawst

AVIATION WEEK
Advantage

4.

5.

iPad 📶   9:41 AM

AVIATION WEEK
& SPACE TECHNOLOGY

MRO Edition

News, Data & Analysis for MRO Management

ENGINES

Raising The Bar

Designing takes center stage as Pratt & Whitney's
geared turbofan and CFM's ...

Guy Norris Ian Diego

CHASING SIERRA NEVADA'S COMMERCIAL SPACE DREAM

AVIATIONWEEK
& SPACE TECHNOLOGY

TOP-PERFORMING AIRLINES
Stars and Survivors

PHANTOM WORKS
Flight-Test Surge

FACE TO FACE
Astrium's
Eric Beranger

6.

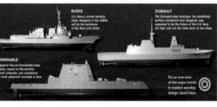

1930

Electronics, a new McGraw-Hill magazine, begins publication.

The book company enters the trade-book field with the Whittlesey House imprint. Its first title is *The World's Economic Dilemma* by Ernest Minor Patterson.

1934

Platt's Oilgram News Service is founded by Warren C. Platt's National Petroleum Publishing Co.

Graham and Dodd's *Security Analysis* is first published. It goes on to become a popular source of insights for investors.

1941

Standard Statistics Co. and Poor's Publishing Co. merge to form Standard & Poor's.

1948

Gregg Publishing Co. becomes part of McGraw-Hill.

Paul Samuelson's classic *Economics* is first published.

1953

McGraw-Hill acquires the forerunners of Platts, which will become a leader in commodities information.

Donald C. McGraw becomes president of McGraw-Hill.

---

tock begins
New York
ge.

Week begins September 7. ouys *Aviation* ch will be thers to
Week.

1931

McGraw-Hill opens its Green Building at 330 West 42nd Street in New York City. It served as world headquarters until 1972.

1935

James H. McGraw Jr. becomes president and chairman of McGraw-Hill.

1945

McGraw-Hill World News Service opens its first foreign bureau, in London.

Dr. Tinsley R. Harrison agrees to develop a new type of medical text, later to be entitled *Harrison's Principles of Internal Medicine.*

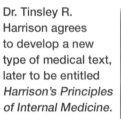

1950

Curtis W. McGraw becomes president and chairman of McGraw-Hill.

THE McGRAW-HILL TIMELINE

1860
Henry Varnum Poor publishes *History of the Railroads and Canals of the United States,* aimed at giving investors insight into the railroad industry.

1892
Frederick W. Dodge begins a construction-project news service and also acquires *Sweet's Real Estate Record & Builder's Guide* and *The Architectural Record.*

1902
The American Machinist Press is incorporated as the Hill Publishing Co. in New York City.

John Robert Gregg publishes *Light-Line Phonography,* the first Gregg shorthand book, in England.

1909
James McGraw and John Hill join their book-publishing departments to form the McGraw-Hill Book Co.

National Petroleum News is founded by Warren C. Platt.

1923
Standard Statistics Co. begins rating general mortgage bonds.

1888
James H. McGraw, a former schoolteacher born in Panama, New York, purchases *The American Journal of Railway Appliances,* a magazine devoted to covering the rail industry.

1897
John A. Hill, a former print-shop apprentice and loco-motive engineer, acquires full interest in the *American Machinist* and sells his part in *Locomotive Engineer,* which he acquired in 1891.

1907
The classic *Standard Handbook for Electrical Engineers* is first pub-lished by the McGraw Publishing Co.

1917
The McGraw and Hill Companies merge to form McGraw-Hill Publishing Co. James H. McGraw serves as president.

The first issue of *Engi-neering News-Record* is published. It is a consoli-dation of the separate Hill and McGraw publications *Engineering News* and *Engineering Record,* respectively.

1929
McGraw-Hill s[...] trading on the Stock Exchan[...]

The Business publication on[...] The company magazine, wh[...] merged with o[...] create *Aviatio[...]*

McGraw Hill Financial

ONE PROUD LEGACY, TWO

McGraw-Hill Education

POWERFUL COMPANIES

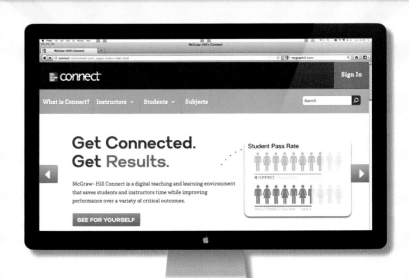

9

REIMAGINE LEARNING

More students. More global. More digital.

That's the future of education. A greater focus on technology, coupled with the rise of emerging markets—and with them millions of new students—marks the greatest opportunity of the 21st century to make education more accessible, affordable, and adaptable, according to McGraw-Hill CEO Harold McGraw III.

"The digitization of education is just huge. McGraw-Hill Education sits right in the heart of one of the biggest opportunities of our time to help young people and professionals learn, grow and succeed literally all over the world," said McGraw.

McGraw-Hill Education's path forward is paved with the successes of the past.

McGraw-Hill's publishing division began with the original intent of focusing on college textbooks and technical handbooks. But in 1932, the company began printing books to serve a wider audience with the introduction of the Whittlesey House imprint, named for founder James H. McGraw's father-in-law, Charles Whittlesey. (Read about McGraw-Hill's popular books in Chapter 11.)

However, it was not until the post-World War II Baby Boom that McGraw-Hill really cemented its presence as a leader in the education industry. In 1952, the company bought the secondary school list of Harper & Brothers, which gave McGraw-Hill a greater presence in vocational and high school education. In 1963, the company acquired Webster Publishing Company, a move that introduced McGraw-Hill into elementary education. The acquisition brought into the McGraw-Hill catalog such classics as William Kottmeyer's *Basic Goals in Spelling*. First published in 1951, it sold its 200 millionth copy in 1984. Generations of students have grown up learning from McGraw-Hill textbooks from kindergarten through college and beyond.

McGraw-Hill has led through innovation from its start in print to the rapid growth of digital learning. The technology of the late 2000s paired with world class educational content and instructional design has offered exciting new opportunities for students to study at their own pace through adaptive learning platforms. That means better feedback and student comprehension and performance.

"From early childhood through professional learning, the education world is changing fast and students and educators are depending on the company they've trusted for years," said Lloyd G. "Buzz" Waterhouse, who was named McGraw-Hill Education president and CEO in June 2012. With all of the company's learning systems now available in digital formats, students and teachers want a way to personalize their education and learn anytime, anywhere.

Recognizing the promise of technology, annual spending for digital educational materials in pre-kindergarten through grade 12 is outpacing spending on textbooks and increased 33 percent in 2010 across the U.S.

"Digital is the future for McGraw-Hill Education and we have a unique chance to lead in this transformation and profoundly affect the lives of students, teachers, and administrators around the world," said Waterhouse. "Together we can all change the way we learn—and thrive."

CINCH Learning is a prime example of how the convergence of technology and McGraw-Hill's content are providing new learning opportunities for students. CINCH Learning is a complete, digital, teacher-led math and science curriculum for grades 6-12 that uses the power of interactive whiteboard teaching to engage students. In early 2012, CINCH Learning recorded strong sales in Texas, providing momentum for later in the year, when it became available nationwide.

CINCH is just one of the products developed at McGraw-Hill Education's Center for Digital Innovation. Established in 2009 in Bothell, Wash., the center is a first-of-a-kind research and development hub with a mission to create leading-edge, paradigm-changing resources to shape the future of education. The center brings together educators, software engineers and digital experts to build on McGraw-Hill Education's vast knowledge and meet the challenges of students in the 21st century.

Perhaps nowhere is the appetite for educational content on digital devices expanding more rapidly than in the professional market, where readers can take advantage of enhanced e-books to interact with and better understand ever-evolving material.

For future doctors and health care professionals around the world, the AccessMedicine platform features online tools that educators can use to assign, manage, and track assignments. The platform was first offered in 2003 and by 2012, AccessMedicine and other McGraw-Hill online medical resources were being used by 87 percent of the medical schools in the U.S. and in more than 65 countries, including Nigeria, Turkey, Saudi Arabia and Singapore.

McGraw-Hill boasts some 6,000 professional e-books available on devices such as Apple's iPad and Amazon's Kindle, 250 mobile applications and an e-book library for institutional clients with unlimited access to 1,000 titles in medicine, business, study skills and more.

1.

2.

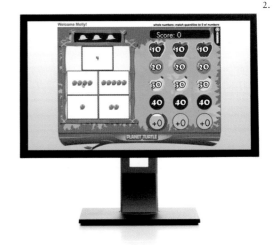

In higher education, one of McGraw-Hill's most popular digital platforms is Connect, a course-management system in use by more than 1.2 million students and educators in 2012. Students can access course content, a multimedia library and e-textbooks, while instructors can assign quizzes, review student performance and give feedback. The program can be accessed with tablets or laptops, so with their regular performance reports, students can see how they are doing anytime, anywhere.

The company is also seeing tremendous success with LearnSmart, an adaptive learning program that guides students through complex material at their own pace as the system measures and monitors their progress. It pinpoints areas where students need more help so instructors can target instruction. If a LearnSmart quiz shows that a student is not absorbing certain material, the program will prompt the student to re-read a particular section and try the quiz again.

LearnSmart helps students succeed by providing a personalized learning path that's based on responses to questions (right or wrong), as well as how confident they feel about the answers they provide. The program also encourages the retention of the material by identifying concepts that students are likely to forget, and directing them back to portions of the e-book to help them solidify concepts.

Such personalization has deep roots in the company. In 1989, the company's College Division, working with Eastman Kodak and R. R. Donnelley, introduced the first computerized publishing system (PRIMIS) that allowed educators to customize a textbook to match their curriculum.

With McGraw-Hill Education's Create, instructors produce customized e-books or printed texts. Educators can pull content from over 4,000 McGraw-Hill Education textbooks, 5,500 articles, 11,000 readings in literature and philosophy, and 25,000 business case studies from such sources as the Harvard Business School. Teachers receive digital proofs almost immediately.

The technological changes affecting learning will reach far into society. For students, adaptive learning technology often means improving performance by at least a letter grade and greater understanding. Dr. Lynda Haas, associate director of composition and course director at the University of California-Irvine, said students using Connect Composition in her classes experience greater gains on their scores.

And teachers spend less time responding to simple language and grammar concerns, and can spend more time on advanced topics, she said.

And for society, all of these advances produce students who

3. College students and educators can manage their courses via McGraw-Hill Education's popular Connect platform.
4. Biology was one of the original high school titles launched by McGraw-Hill Education in 2012 designed specifically for Apple's iPad tablet.

3.

4.

are better prepared and can better compete in the global knowledge economy.

"Technology enables students to touch, spin and explore the structure of a molecule as they're reading about it in a text, watch a speech by Dr. Martin Luther King, Jr. as they read about the civil rights era—and ask questions of their classmates and complete their homework assignments all in a digital environment. By fostering these connections, technology can enhance and increase students' learning interactions, leading to better performance," said Stephen Laster, Chief Digital Officer.

"Customers come to us for advice. Our solutions are second to none and our people are the best in the industry," Waterhouse said. "Our brand is known for excellence, and we are becoming a truly global company."

It was partly because of the need for greater focus and investment to drive innovation globally that the Board of Directors of McGraw-Hill, following a year-long portfolio review, decided in 2011 to create two powerful new companies: McGraw Hill Financial and McGraw-Hill Education. In 2012, the company announced a deal to sell McGraw-Hill Education to Apollo Global Management.

"We are excited about what this means for McGraw-Hill Education," Waterhouse said. "Apollo is a leading global alternative investment manager and its affiliated funds have made significant investments in learning companies for more than a decade. McGraw-Hill Education's expertise and premier brands coupled with Apollo's resources represent a powerful combination."

As the education market evolves and the company changes with it, its mission and values remain the same: to share knowledge and educate the world. The trends are going McGraw-Hill Education's way. For example, the value of an education is becoming increasingly clear—and necessary. In 2011, lifetime earnings were estimated to be 2.8 times higher for someone with a higher education degree compared to someone with only a high school diploma. In 1980, that ratio was 1.7 times higher.

Enrollment is rising. In the U.S., enrollment in pre-kindergarten through grade 8 is projected to reach 41.7 million students in 2020, from about 38.7 million in 2010. Higher education is growing too. Enrollment in degree-granting institutions rose from 14.5 million students in 1994 to 20.7 million students in 2009. And it's expected to reach 23 million students by 2020. As student enrollments grew year after year in the 20th century, the company made targeted investments. In 1989 it created a joint venture with Macmillan, combining the company's kindergarten-12th grade units. (Four years later, it bought out Macmillan's shares.) In 2000, the company acquired Tribune Education, a highly regarded educational publisher with strength in language arts, math, foreign language, social studies, health, English, reading, educational software and teacher training spanning pre-K through college and professional markets.

India, China, Brazil, as well as a number of nations in the Middle East, are seeing enormous economic growth and financial success. The so-called BRICS countries (Brazil, Russia, India, China and South Africa) are seeing particular growth and are a key focus. These countries' combined share of the world GDP rose from 16 percent to 25 percent from 2000 to 2010. In terms of global GDP growth from 2000 to 2008, these countries accounted for 55 percent.

> ## "Customers come to us for advice. Our solutions are second to none and our people are the best in the industry."
> ### —Lloyd G. "Buzz" Waterhouse, CEO of McGraw-Hill Education

As their economies grow so has demand for better-educated workers. And as these countries become more prosperous, experts expect their spending on education to increase. India, China and Brazil combined have eight times more students than the U.S. India, in particular, is a huge opportunity for McGraw-Hill as its 1.2 billion citizens understand the value of education and a growing middle class increasingly seeks it out. The value India places in education can be seen in the country's more than 31,000 higher education systems, far outpacing the 6,700 in the U.S. and 4,300 in China.

To meet the global demand for knowledge, the company is eyeing key partnerships around the world. In India, McGraw-Hill Education's Campus to Career program helps students become employment-ready in a variety of fields with a curriculum ranging from quantitative aptitude, to reasoning to resume writing and interviewing. In China, McGraw-Hill Education introduced a comprehensive curriculum for a groundbreaking after-school program that will potentially touch more than 500,000 students. The program, developed in partnership with the New Oriental Education & Technology Group, helps students develop the skills they need to succeed in a Western higher education environment and in virtually any career in the world.

"As more students in China go beyond the nation's borders to study and work, it is essential that they develop the language and critical thinking skills they need to compete and collaborate successfully," said Philip Ruppel, president, McGraw-Hill Education International & Professional. He sees opportunities for McGraw-Hill Education to leverage the program in other countries in the future. Global expansion and digitization certainly are creating exciting opportunities for McGraw-Hill Education.

On Left: LearnSmart guides higher education students through complex material through its adaptive learning capabilities. **Below:** McGraw-Hill Networks is an award-winning learning system for social studies in grades 6-12 that brings abstract concepts to life.

10

HELPING TEACHERS HELP STUDENTS

Teachers can make the perfect lesson plans, engage their students and administer diagnostic tests. But there is value in assessing progress beyond a report card. How do educators, districts, and states know how well their students are learning—and how do they compare with students elsewhere? The answer is educational assessments, which are becoming an integral part of learning. They gauge the progress of each student as well as the overall academic achievement.

The use of assessments is growing and should continue with the increasing need for education in places such as China, Brazil and the Middle East. This growth has spurred the business of CTB/McGraw-Hill, which ranks among education's leading assessment partners. The company serves pre-college education and adult basic education around the world, by providing assessment programs and services with innovative delivery, reporting, scoring and data management services. Its long time motto succinctly explains its purpose: "Help the teacher help the child."

CTB began life in 1926 as the Research Service Co., soon renamed the California Test Bureau. Dr. Willis Clark, assistant director of research for the Los Angeles public schools, designed tests and as his tests' effectiveness spread, other cities' schools became interested in using them. That prompted Clark's wife, Ethel, to begin an enterprise to make them available. She first acquired publication rights to the tests and then sent out word of their availability to administrators in 25 cities. One of the first subscribers, Kansas City, soon placed an order for 20,000 tests.

Tests in the fundamentals of arithmetic were followed by the Progressive Achievement Test (1933) and the California Test of Mental Maturity (1936), which measured academic skills including logical and numerical reasoning, spatial relationships, verbal concepts, and memory. In 1938, CTB turned to computerized test scoring, made possible by IBM's development of the Type 805 Test Scoring Machine, which processed answer sheets 10 times faster than humans could. The computer "was as big as a desk," recalled the Clarks' daughter, June Duran Stock. "The graphite [from pencil marks] produced a little electric charge, which was indicated on a volt meter."

By the end of the 1930s, CTB had moved into personality testing, a popular phenomenon of the mid-20th century. First came the California Test of Personality, which produced a "social adjustment score" that helped teachers understand students' self-assurance, independence, and other social skills. This led to a participation in the world of work, notably with the company's Personnel Selection and Classification Test, which measured not only job applicants' reading and math skills but also their reliability and aptitude for working with others.

By 1965, when McGraw-Hill acquired CTB, the company had annual sales of $3 million. While CTB's tests had been regularly revised and updated, McGraw-Hill helped the outfit develop the Criterion Referenced Tests, which were intended to be more diagnostic, helping teachers better employ their materials and make instruction more individualized.

In that decade, too, to make sure the tests fairly assessed students of all races and backgrounds, the company recruited civil rights advocate Dr. D. Ross Green, who established procedures to ensure the tests were fair.

Through the years, CTB has continued to help educators assess the progress of students of every age across the United States and internationally. In the 1980s, as there was a growing number of American students whose first language was Spanish, the company created an achievement battery in that language to assess basic reading and math skills.

Developments have continued as the need for such measurements has become more nuanced. In 1996, CTB incorporated the California Achievement Tests and the California Test of Basic Skills into an innovative assessment series called TerraNova. Writing Roadmap, introduced in 2003, is an online writing assessment tool that allows students to practice and improve their writing skills and gives teachers the ability to measure and track proficiency.

An update introduced in 2012 included all-new natural language processing and artificial intelligence to automate the essay scoring process. CTB said this will allow teachers to include dramatically more student writing activities each year and save some 100 hours or more of grading per year.

And in 2006, CTB introduced Acuity, an award-winning assessment program that can be delivered via pencil and paper, online, or through student-response devices or "clickers." CTB's Online Reporting System provides

1.

2.

3.

4.

> **"Students have always been our inspiration, ever since Ethel Clark sent out a series of penny postcards inviting school districts to use CTB's newly developed assessments in 1926."**
> —**CTB President Ellen Haley**

educators and parents with the information to measurably improve student performance. The online component with Acuity marked a first for the industry in terms of making such measurements online.

By 2012, CTB served more than 18 million students across the United States and in 49 countries. The number is expected to grow as the demand for education surges worldwide in coming decades. "Students have always been our inspiration, ever since Ethel Clark sent out a series of penny postcards inviting school districts to use CTB's newly developed assessments in 1926," said CTB President Ellen Haley.

5.

6.

7.

5. Writing Roadmap, introduced in 2003, helps teachers track student progress.
6. CTB Personnel Tests helped employers evaluate prospective employees.
7. An ad touting an expansion of CTB's personality testing to range from first grade through college students and adults.

LEONARDO DA VINCI

THE MADRID CODICES
NATIONAL LIBRARY MADRID

VOLUME II
FACSIMILE EDITION
OF
CODEX MADRID II

ORIGINAL SPANISH TITLE:
TRATADOS VARIOS DE FORTIFICACION ESTATICA Y GEOMETRIA ESCRITOS EN ITALIANO
LIBRARY NUMBER 8936

1974

McGRAW-HILL BOOK COMPANY

UNDER THE AUSPICES
OF THE
**GENERAL DIRECTORATE
OF ARCHIVES
AND LIBRARIES OF MADRID**
SPAIN

PRINTED IN SWITZERLAND
BY C. J. BUCHER, LUCERNE
BOUND BY
GROSSBUCHBINDEREI SIGLOCH
KÜNZELSAU, GERMANY

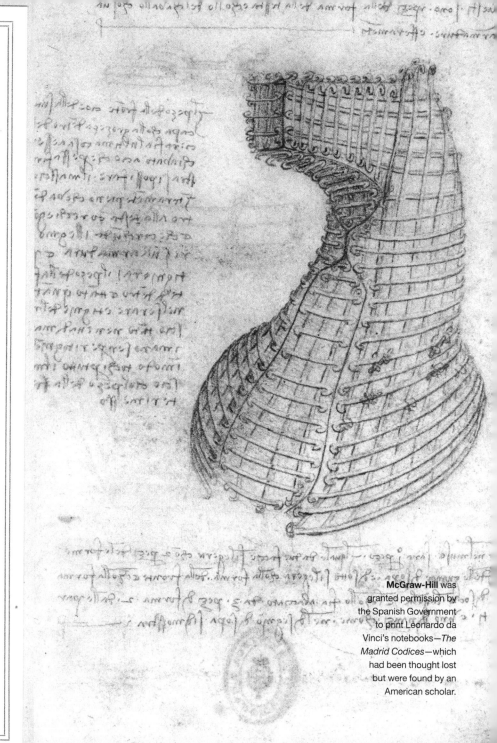

McGraw-Hill was granted permission by the Spanish Government to print Leonardo da Vinci's notebooks—*The Madrid Codices*—which had been thought lost but were found by an American scholar.

11

BOOKS THROUGH THE YEARS

From a regal lion taking a walk through a village, to what's seen as the seminal book for mechanical engineers. From recipes by Betty Crocker to notebooks by Leonardo da Vinci, McGraw-Hill has published works covering nearly every topic imaginable through the years.

And over many years the publishing house has handled a wide range of authors, from General Douglas MacArthur, to black militant Eldridge Cleaver, and celebrated writer Vladimir Nabokov.

"When I came on board in 1965, it was one of the strongest trade houses with a complete line of children's books, bestselling novels, biographies, histories, and so forth," recalled National Accounts Manager Michel Spitzer.

Successes were many over the years. In 1954, the company published Louise Fatio's *The Happy Lion*, a children's book that was chosen as one of the 10 best illustrated picture books of the year by the *New York Times*. Six sequels and a movie followed, with over a million total copies in print in 13 languages. In her tale, a gentle if imposing King of Beasts walks through a French village after a zookeeper accidentally leaves his cage door unlatched. Citizens faint and flee, all very much to the surprise of the beast.

"I can't think what makes them do that," said the Happy Lion. "They are always so polite at the zoo."

Marks' *Standard Handbook for Mechanical Engineers*, another top seller, has been in print since 1916 and revised 11 times since its first publication. And then there's the 20-volume, 13,000-page *The Encyclopedia of Science and Technology*, which has sold over 3 million copies since its initial publication in 1961.

Benjamin Graham and David L. Dodd's *Security Analysis*, first published by McGraw-Hill in 1934, forever changed the theory and practice of successful investing. Written in the midst of the Great Depression and in the wake of the 1929 stock market crash, the book convinced the nation that stocks were still worth buying and became a bible for generations of investors, including Warren Buffett. Indeed Buffett, perhaps the world's most famous—and successful—investor wrote a foreword for a publication marking the 75th anniversary of the book in 2008.

"I studied from *Security Analysis* while I was at Columbia in 1950-1951, when I had the extraordinary good luck to have Ben Graham and Dave Dodd as teachers. Together, the book and the men changed my life," Buffett said.

But it wasn't all business and technical writing for McGraw-Hill. Humorist and newspaper columnist Erma Bombeck brought comedy and insight to readers in titles that included *The Grass Is Always*

 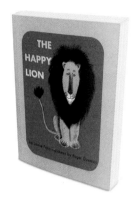 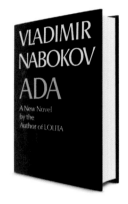  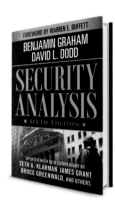

Greener Over the Septic Tank (1976) and *If Life Is a Bowl of Cherries, What Am I Doing in the Pits?* (1978).

And of course, there was *Betty Crocker's Picture Cook Book* (1950), considered the standard of cookbooks for decades to follow. It covered everything from meal planning to appetizers, cream soups, casseroles and desserts and was much beloved for its pictures, which showed a whole generation how to cook. When the book was published in 1950, its sales rivaled those of the Bible and by 1952 it was in its seventh printing and had sold more than 2 million copies, according to TheDailyMeal.com.

Intellectual pursuits also figured prominently too. Nobel Prize winner Heinrich Böll published several modernist works of fiction, including *Billiards at Half-Past Nine* (1962) and *Eighteen Stories* (1966).

Overall McGraw-Hill claims approximately 50 Nobel Prize winners as authors, including Paul Samuelson, who won the Nobel in 1970 in Economics. His book *Economics* is considered the seminal book of its kind. (To learn more, see Chapter 12.) Of those Nobel Prize winners, some 38 have been published in AccessScience and in the *Encyclopedia of Science and Technology*.

Other top titles include Harvard President James B. Conant weighing in with numerous influential examinations of public education, including *The American High School*

Today (1959). Techno-analyst Marshall McLuhan offered the cult-inspiring *Understanding Media: The Extensions of Man* (1964) and *War and Peace in the Global Village* (1968). *The Encyclopedia of World Art* (1962) provided a panorama of artistic achievement.

Celebrated author Vladimir Nabokov was one of the company's more prolific writers, having published *The Annotated Lolita* (1970), *Ada* (1969) and *Strong Opinions* (1973), among other titles, over the years.

A series of titles drew upon unearthed writings of Samuel Johnson biographer James Boswell, including the 1950 publication, *Boswell's London Journal, 1762-1763*. And perhaps taking the prize for high-culture achievement was Leonardo da Vinci's five-volume, red-leather-bound *The Madrid Codices* (1974), which drew upon the Renaissance artist's notebooks that had been discovered in the National Library in Madrid.

There were also many works of topical interest. The very first of the company's trade books, or volumes intended for the general public, was Ernest Minor Patterson's *The World's Economic Dilemma* (1930), published under the Whittlesey House imprint. A rash of lively works came in the 1960s: *P.T. 109* (1961), by Robert Donovan, detailed the World War II heroics of newly elected President John F. Kennedy. *Fail Safe* (1962) by journalists Eugene Burdick and Harvey Wheeler,

> "I studied from *Security Analysis* while I was at Columbia in 1950-1951, when I had the extraordinary good luck to have Ben Graham and Dave Dodd as teachers. Together, the book and the men changed my life."
>
> **— Warren Buffett, famed investor**

raised the specter of an accidental nuclear war. Novelist Robert Ruark's *Uhuru* (1962) considered recently liberated African societies. Civil rights leader Whitney Young analyzed American life in *Beyond Racism* (1969). Ron Kovic's *Born on the Fourth of July* (1976) gave voice to the traumatizing experience of Vietnam veterans. And in social commentary, it would be hard to top Black Panther Party leader Eldridge Cleaver's *Soul On Ice* (1968) or Germaine Greer's feminist manifesto, *The Female Eunuch* (1971).

The company's thousands of titles now focus primarily on education for all levels and professional books, such as studies on the success of businessman and former Apple CEO Steve Jobs, self-help and health books, and language instruction books.

A LEGACY BEGINS AT LUNCH

McGRAW

HILL

Meals lead to deals in business—and in the case of McGraw-Hill, one particular lunch fostered the beginnings of a global powerhouse. Lunch amid the rococo splendor of Haan's Restaurant on New York's Park Row was the setting for the 1909 brainstorm that was the making of the McGraw-Hill Book Co.

Between courses, Edward Caldwell of the McGraw Publishing Co. and Martin Foss of Hill Publishing agreed on the cost advantages of linking their respective companies' book-publishing operations. For each company, books were just a sideline—an outgrowth of their main business of publishing technical and trade magazines. Each had been taking articles that originated in such journals

as *Electrochemical Industry* or *Power* and turning them into hardcovers for their readers' reference shelves. A merged book company could draw articles from all of the McGraw and Hill magazines, realize efficiencies of scale, and save on duplicative salaries, advertising, and catalogs. Existing net profits for the two outfits were small in 1908—$14,000 for McGraw and $11,000 for Hill. Together, their profits could be even larger.

Neither James McGraw nor John Hill, heads of their companies, liked the idea at first. But each came around to the Caldwell-Foss plan. And in July 1909, the McGraw-Hill Book Company opened its doors with a staff of 12 employees. A coin toss determined that Mc-

Graw's name would go first on the door. The company's first catalog listed 200 titles, and in its first year, it sold around 73,000 books.

The book company's first titles were very similar to the magazines' content: Future U.S. President Herbert Hoover's *Principles of Mining* (1909) was one of the first volumes to carry the new McGraw-Hill colophon. The company's first series, in 1910, was *Electrical Engineering Texts*, and in 1911 Charles Proteus of General Electric contributed his seminal *Engineering Mathematics*. Soon to come were *The Practice of Copper Smelting* (1911), by Edward Dyer Peters, and Dexter Kimball's *Principles of Industrial Organization* (1913).

By 1930, the company had branched out, establishing an imprint for more popular books, Whittlesey House. Its first great success: Walter B. Pitkin's humorous *Life Begins at Forty*, a 1932 best-seller.

Professor and McGraw-Hill author Paul **Samuelson** wins the Nobel Prize in Economics in 1970.

12

MACRO UNDERSTANDING: BRINGING ECONOMICS TO THE MASSES

It would, he hoped, awaken students like "the kiss of the prince in *Sleeping Beauty*."

He also hoped, of course, that his book would sell.

But neither Massachusetts Institute of Technology professor Paul Samuelson nor his book publisher would have dared to dream of the success ultimately enjoyed by his seminal textbook, *Economics*, first published in 1948. More than 60 years later, in its 19th edition, the volume has sold around 20 million copies around the globe and been translated into more than 40 languages.

In his early 30s, and recently awarded the John Bates Clark Award as the best economist under 40, Samuelson in 1945 turned his hand to textbook-writing. He spent three years laboring on the book while teaching a heavy course load. His goal: To make the revolutionary ideas of British economist John Maynard Keynes accessible via clear writing, simple diagrams, and compelling, up-to-date examples.

Samuelson was guided by his own college experience. There was, he felt, a huge gap between the theory-laden material he'd been taught and the problems of the real world. "Why should teachers of economics withhold from the first-year course the really interesting and vital problems of over-all economic policy" in favor of simple instruction in, say, supply and demand, he wondered?

Samuelson was courted by numerous publishers, including Alfred A. Knopf, Macmillan, Prentice-Hall, and McGraw-Hill. He once said that he decided to go with McGraw-Hill because of editor Basil Dandison, whom he called "a true gentleman." It didn't hurt, moreover, that McGraw-Hill was the publisher of *Business Cycles* by Samuelson's mentor, Joseph A. Schumpeter.

Dandison had risen through the ranks at McGraw-Hill, working as a "college traveler"—or sales rep and talent scout—before becoming an editor. While Samuelson was still shopping the book, Dandison volunteered to poll college professors, getting their reactions to Samuelson's approach. "I'd like to learn if a little flippancy would be acceptable," said Samuelson. No, sorry, said the straitlaced guardians of the science. But, it turned out, they were ready for a book rooted in Lord Keynes' theories.

Within four years of its first publication, *Economics* had sold over 120,000 copies, far outdistancing earlier texts by the likes of F.W. Taussig and Richard T. Ely. Every three or four years, Samuelson would revise his book, and its sales inched ever upwards.

Those revisions proved essential to the volume's steady and unparalleled sales. When he first wrote the book, readers were focused on unemployment. The third and fourth editions were more concerned with inflation, and by 1970, there was growing concern over problems of inequality and race. The author also took account of changing fashions in the discipline of economics, offering explanations of Milton Friedman's monetarism and the supply-and-demand-theory skepticism of John Kenneth Galbraith.

The volume's real-world relevance drew kudos from colleagues and reviewers alike. "The tragedy of economics instruction in the U.S. has been that students were so little exposed to the ideas and issues that were agitating the real world," said an early review in *Fortune*. "This will hardly be the fate of a student who studies this book."

In 1970, Samuelson was awarded the Nobel Prize in Economics, honored "for the scientific work through which he has developed static and dynamic economic theory and actively contributed to raising the level of analysis in economic science."

Ten years later, with Samuelson nearing retirement, the publisher decided that the book was in need of a general overhaul. Students, it was felt, were less likely to have enjoyed the classical education that the author had presupposed, and regular additions of new material had caused the book to take on an unwanted girth. Yale professor William D. Nordhaus, who became a co-author, took on the task of paring down and restructuring the work. Newer editions would place greater emphasis on global developments and evolving economic analysis. In later years, the text was accompanied by software that offered electronic problem-solving tools.

"The book's core coverage remains the same," said Douglas Reiner, Managing Director of Higher Education. "It's the policy applications that keep getting updated." Other additions include material on economic growth and questions of consumer and producer surplus.

Could a modern-day book duplicate Samuelson's success? Reiner observes that McGraw-Hill itself has other entrants in the field, including another top-selling book, *Economics* by Campbell McConnell, Stanley Brue, and Sean Flynn. "But it would be hard for any book today to achieve similar total sales, particularly since Samuelson was really the only book of its kind from 1948 to 1960," Reiner said.

In December 2009, Samuelson died. Princeton economist Paul Krugman wrote in his blog in the *New York Times*: "It's hard to convey the full extent of Samuelson's greatness. Most economists would love to have written even one seminal paper—a paper that fundamentally changes the way people think about some issue. Samuelson wrote dozens: from international trade to finance to growth theory to speculation to well, just about everything, underlying much of what we know is a key Samuelson paper that set the agenda for generations of scholars."

Dr. Tinsley R. Harrison was editor-in-chief of the bestselling reference book in medicine, *Harrison's Principles of Internal Medicine.*

13

A SEMINAL MEDICAL TEXT

Dr. Tinsley R. Harrison was taught to revere his father's mentor. Yet he would write a seminal textbook that would eclipse that mentor's work. A case of intellectual patricide?

In 1892, the British-born, Baltimore-based physician William Osler authored the first modern textbook of internal medicine, *The Principles and Practice of Medicine*. Not until the closing decades of the 19th century had doctors been able to begin compiling a systematic "nosography," or catalog of diseases. Moreover, thanks to advances in bacteriology, they were now able to assign specific causes to common illnesses.

Osler's ambition was, in his own words, "to wrest from nature the secrets which have perplexed philosophers in all ages [and] to track to their sources the causes of disease." His book was a tremendous success, becoming a standard text in medical schools.

But much like a rival work, Dr. Russell Cecil's *The Cecil Textbook of Medicine* (1927), Osler's effort was awkwardly organized, grouping "disease entities" according to their origins.

It was not until 1950 that a book with a more practical organization appeared. Dr. Tinsley R. Harrison's *Harrison's Principles of Internal Medicine* took the radical step of grouping maladies according to their symptoms. A key section entitled "Cardinal Manifestations of Disease" included entries on headache, back and neck pain, fever, and much more. Moreover, unlike Osler's work, Harrison's was a compilation written by dozens of specialists.

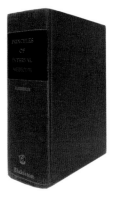
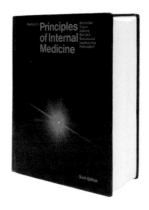

"No greater opportunity, responsibility, or obligation can fall to the lot of a human being than to become a physician," Harrison wrote. And he reminded his readers to bear in mind that the patient had turned to them, "fearful and hopeful, seeking relief, help, and reassurance."

Harrison was the son of a doctor, Groce Harrison, who as a student had befriended Osler, a teacher at Johns Hopkins Medical School. Such was Groce's lifelong regard for Osler that his son claimed as a child to have been unable to distinguish between God, Jesus Christ, and the Baltimore professor.

Tinsley himself attended medical school at Johns Hopkins and after serving in positions at various institutions, he became chair of medicine at the Medical College of Alabama in the same year that he published the first edition of *Harrison's Principles of Internal Medicine*.

Although Tinsley Harrison died in 1978, his work lives on thanks to new generations of writers and editors, including such notables as legendary cardiologist Eugene Braunwald of Boston's Brigham and Women's Hospital and Harvard Medical School and Anthony Fauci, the

"No greater opportunity, responsibility, or obligation can fall to the lot of a human being than to become a physician."
—Dr. Tinsley R. Harrison, editor-in-chief of *Harrison's Principles of Internal Medicine*

director of the National Institutes of Allergy and Infectious Diseases. Over the decades, *Harrison's* has become "the benchmark for textbooks of internal medicine," in the words of The Journal of the American Medical Association. It has been translated into 16 languages and is widely used in Europe, Latin America, and Asia—especially in India.

By 1984, *Harrison's* represented the work of more than 200 specialists and contained more than 2,000 pages. In 2011, McGraw-Hill

  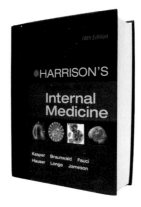 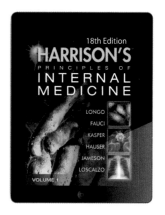

published the 18th edition of the work. That edition consists of two volumes created by about 500 contributors, containing over 2,700 pages, scores of full-color images, a DVD supplement with dozens of videos, and 57 additional e-chapters.

Later revisions and additions cover such contemporary concerns as the demographics of aging, the impact of genes on cancer development, bioterrorism and clinical medicine, and neuropsychiatric problems among war veterans.

As technology and the medical field have taken a more digital focus, so too has *Harrison's*. An enhanced e-book version has been developed for tablet devices such as the iPad. The subscription-based *Harrison's Online* includes the full text of the printed book along with frequent updates, audio recordings and podcasts, and an expanded collection of clinical photos.

Need instant reference? *Harrison's Practice*, a Web, wireless, and PDA resource launched in 2006 offers point-of-care information to such primary care providers as internists, residents, and nurse practitioners. The company also offers *Harrison's Self-Assessment and Board Review*, a study guide for medical students.

The *Harrison's* line of titles is complemented by McGraw-Hill's expanding group of subscription-based sites delivering information on such specialties as pharmacy, surgery, pediatrics, and anesthesiology. AccessMedicine is a vast network of clinical resources, including such well-established titles as *Tintinalli's Emergency Medicine* and *Williams Hematology*. And JAMAEvidence offers tools for teaching and applying evidence-based medicine.

But *Harrison's* remains the gold standard.

"It is the bestselling reference book in medicine," said Scott Grillo, vice president and publisher of McGraw-Hill's medical group. "It is one of the most widely recognized and respected brands in the field."

Above: *Harrison's Principles of Internal Medicine* through the years, including the first edition at left through the 18th edition in 2011. In a review, the *Journal of the American Medical Association* called it "a book that remains as fundamental to current medical practice as the first edition was in 1949."

THE BUSINESS WEEK

FOR THE WEEK ENDING SEPTEMBER 7, 1929

A McGRAW-HILL PUBLICATION
15 CENTS

A McGraw-Hill Publication

BusinessWeek

June 30, 1980 • $1.50

SPECIAL ISSUE

THE REINDUSTRIALIZATION OF AMERICA

On Left: The first edition of what was then known as *The Business Week*, published in 1929. **On Right:** A notable special issue from 1980.

14

NOT JUST NEWS, INTELLIGENCE

Lew Young slammed his fist down on the mahogany desk. "The *old BusinessWeek*?" he said. "Not one of those stories would be allowed in *my* magazine," he said.

End of discussion.

The editor-in-chief of *BusinessWeek* between the late 1960s and the mid-1980s was famous for his headstrong personality.

And through his decisive, determined actions, Young reshaped business journalism. Stories should take a stand, uncover trends, and have "forward spin," or an orientation to the future, he instructed. He didn't care for lively writing, and in fact viewed it with suspicion, as if it were a mere disguise for poor reporting. He wanted news accounts to tell not only what happened, but *why* it happened.

Once Young became editor, in 1969, *BusinessWeek* began giving more coverage to information processing and telecommunications. The magazine also began paying greater attention to Asia, particularly Japan, and to social issues. In 1975, it won a National Magazine Award for its coverage of problems faced by women in the workplace.

The achievements paid off: Circulation worldwide rose from 633,000 to 856,000 during his tenure.

Young was only one of the many prescient editors and professional staffers who transformed *BusinessWeek* into one of America's most important periodicals—respected by business leaders and business skeptics alike, often cited by politicians, pundits, and U.S. presidents.

From its beginning, the publication was awash in news. The year of *BusinessWeek's* birth was an eventful one. In its first issue, the magazine observed: "Stock prices are generally out of line with safe earnings expectations, and the market is almost wholly 'psychological'—irregular, unsteady, and properly apprehensive of the inevitable readjustment that draws near."

The warning came on September 7, 1929. One month later, the Great Crash flattened stock prices. The Great Depression was on.

Despite all the news going on at that time, *The Business Week*— renamed simply *BusinessWeek* in 1934—spent the first decades of its life as one of many publications devoted to leisurely reading, with such

articles as "Dry Ice Finds Many New Uses" and "Skirts Come Down, Trade Picks Up." Early covers were artsy: full-color illustrations of steamships and airships, loading docks and steel production.

The periodical began to find its feet in the 1930s. According to longtime publisher Colonel Willard Chevalier, it became increasingly evident that "what we wanted was a fast-moving, weekly news magazine that had a particular slant for the businessman." Charts and graphs began appearing throughout the publication, and on the cover, a standing element began appearing: the "business indicator," a thermometer gauge that purported to tell the "temperature" of current business activity. On April 26, 1947, for example, the Business Week Index thermometer stood at 195, 20 points higher than the level of a year earlier, reflecting such factors as increased steel production, burgeoning residential-building contracts, and higher electric-power output. The business indicator would continue to run on the magazine's cover into the mid-1950s.

Increasingly, news was the magazine's mainstay. A 1939 issue carried an analysis of U.S. Supreme Court decisions likely to affect business. In 1942, there appeared an organizational chart of "Who Runs the War Effort," and by June of 1945, articles on reconversion of war industries dominated, appearing alongside photos of "Ford's first postwar passenger car."

That postwar boom gave *BusinessWeek* its biggest boost—and an incentive to further define itself. Standing departments such as International Outlook, Finance, Aviation, and Labor appeared. In 1947, a Business Abroad column considered "What's Ahead for Turkey?" And an editorial inveighed against treating the steel industry's 15 cents-per-hour wage increase as a pattern to be emulated by all of industry. Moreover, observes Jack Dierdorff, who began at the magazine in 1956 and served in many positions including managing editor: "The big change in my time came under Elliot Bell, who made *BusinessWeek* the first magazine to cover economics seriously." Bell served as editor and publisher from 1950 through 1967. His economics reports, created along with economics editor Leonard Silk (later of the *New York Times*), were cited by no less than President Lyndon Johnson.

Young came to *BusinessWeek* following stints at McGraw-Hill trade publications *Product Engineering* and *Electronics*, and at Westinghouse Corp. In 1984, he resigned. His successor, who had served as executive editor for only two years, could hardly have been more different.

Stephen B. Shepard came to *BusinessWeek* after working as editor at the *Saturday Review*, a magazine best-remembered for its erudite and witty columns penned by former editor Norman Cousins. Shepard had worked at *BusinessWeek* as a reporter for 10 years beginning in the mid-1960s, then moved on to Columbia University and *Newsweek* before returning.

By comparison with Young, Shepard was collegial and easygoing, although he certainly had a point of view. He emphasized improved writing, with a focus on personalities and storytelling. He stressed breaking news, and a modern, four-color design of the magazine. And thanks to Young, said Shepard, "when computerization and the Internet revolution took off, we had a head start." Shepard beefed up the Silicon Valley bureau, finance coverage, and the magazine's global reach, with 27 international bureaus at the peak. In 1981, an international edition of the magazine appeared, with advertising tailored to separate European, Latin American, and Asian markets. In the late 1980s and '90s, there were Chinese, Polish, Hungarian, and Russian-language editions.

In the 1990s, *BusinessWeek* won two National Magazine Awards for General Excellence, along with a top award for the story "The Quality Imperative." A "best business schools" franchise would be widely coveted and imitated. Investigation of a "New Economy"—one featuring a high-tech engine and markedly higher productivity—stoked debate and controversy.

And by the turn of the 21st century, with circulation up by 40%, to 1.2 million, *BusinessWeek* had become the world's most widely read business magazine.

In 1994, *BusinessWeek* went digital, becoming a feature on web portal America Online. Two years later came the debut of the magazine's own website, businessweek.com, made up of all the articles that appeared in the print magazine plus stock quotes and a growing number of original stories, podcasts, and videos. In 2000, *BusinessWeek Online* won the National Magazine Award for General Excellence in New Media. In 2005, Shepard retired after 20 years as editor-in-chief, and Stephen J. Adler, a *Wall Street Journal* deputy managing editor, was named as replacement.

This successful periodical had survived the Great Depression, numerous wars, and the September 11, 2001 attacks, and by 2000 had 6,000 total pages of advertising. But with the economic downturn of the late 2000s, a new focus on digital publications and consumers receiving their news on mobile devices, advertising fell across the magazine industry. In 2009, McGraw-Hill found the magazine a new home at Bloomberg L.P., which became more focused on business news as McGraw-Hill focused on growing its famous analytics and benchmark brands.

Top left page: *BusinessWeek* editor-in-chief Lew Young (center left) interviews President Jimmy Carter in 1978. **Bottom left:** Steve Shepard, then editor-in-chief of *BusinessWeek*, in 1985. **1.** The magazine in 1935. **2.** A 2001 issue of *BusinessWeek/ China*. **3.** The first edition after the attacks on Sept. 11, 2001. **4.** An online edition of *BusinessWeek*.

1.

2.

3.

4.

McGRAW-HILL ANNOUNCES

electronics
electron tubes—their radio, audio
visio and industrial applications

15
CAPTURING LIGHTNING
IN A MAGAZINE

"When a small computer moves into the home, it will plan, schedule and control meal preparation and program the cleaning operations. It will record and remind the householder of all social engagements; teach the children; and finally calculate and pay the income taxes."

That was the vision from the April 1965 edition of *Electronics*, a periodical that McGraw-Hill published between 1930 and 1988. It is in the nature of tech magazines to appeal to the public's desire for a "gee-whiz" experience, and *Electronics* was no exception. In 1965, computerization was still in its relative infancy and home computers were all but nonexistent.

Thirty-five years earlier, at the time of the magazine's inaugural issue, it was electron tubes that made technology-lovers' hearts race.

"The applications are almost infinite with the three kinds of tubes," wrote inventor Thomas Alva Edison in the magazine's first issue. "They open a field for research in physics, chemistry, electricity, heat and light, beyond imagination."

In a decade, vacuum tubes had become the basis for a billion-dollar industry. A lengthy list of applications ran on the magazine's cover: "radio, sound pictures, telephony, broadcasting...beam transmission, photo-electric cells . . . automatic processing, crime detection, geophysics," and on and on.

It's hard to imagine now, but in 1930, the very term "electronics" was rarely heard. "The word ELECTRONICS has had little if any place in electrical engineering nomenclature," observed a 1929 corporate memo discussing the magazine. But it seemed to suit the new publication as it was "all-embracive of the paper's function."

McGraw-Hill's magazine helped popularize the term, and from its changing content one can trace the evolution of the field.

For many years, the articles in *Electronics* were not for the general public. Instead, they were written for an audience of engineers and sophisticated executives. Included in the first issue were articles such as "The Power Pentode, Its Characteristics and Applications," the equation-rich "Tuned Radio-Frequency Amplifiers," and a two-page sampling of new products, including a light-intensity meter from Westinghouse and an elevator-car control system from General Electric.

In the 1940s, military matters predominated, with such articles as "Radar Development" and "The Technical Basis of Atomic Explosives." Postwar manpower shortages were addressed in "Planning for Automatic Process Control." And there was increasing interest in television. As early as 1938, the magazine's editors constructed a model television receiver in their offices. By August of 1951 they were publishing articles on "Plans for Compatible Color Television" and "Picture Generator for Color Television."

Transistors and space exploration also made good copy. A 1949 issue featured transistor inventor William Shockley and others on the cover, while a 1964 issue considered "Dolling Up a Space Probe."

In 1965, *Electronics* published what would become its most famous article: "Cramming More Components onto Integrated Circuits" by Intel co-founder Gordon E. Moore, in which the executive introduced what would become well-known as Moore's Law. In essence, Moore declared

that falling costs were allowing the number of transistors on a chip to double every two years. The result, he correctly predicted, would be a proliferation of ever smaller and ever more powerful devices.

Electronics' readership rose steadily. In its first year, the magazine had a circulation of 5,000, rising to 33,000 by 1950 and 52,000 by 1960. Beginning as a monthly publication, *Electronics* was a weekly for a time beginning in 1958, then made a move over to a bi-weekly publication as readers seemed unable to keep up.

In the uncertain 1970s, *Electronics* began helping readers with career considerations, notably with a look at the state of the engineering profession.

"The future belongs to a tough breed of generalists who can handle four or five engineering careers in a lifetime," a special report noted. The future looked best for those with a background in "computer-aided design," it continued.

In the 1980s, the magazine returned to a weekly publication schedule and its title changed to *Electronics Week* and then *Electronics: The Worldwide Technology Weekly*. Articles began taking on a more accessible, business-oriented tone, as with "How Philips Sweated the Cost Out of its Scopes" and "Can IBM's New Laptop Build a Volume Market," both from April of 1986. In that year, circulation rose to 93,000.

But the future belonged to more specialized publications, from *Technology Review* to *Wired*. In 1988, McGraw-Hill sold *Electronics* to Dutch publisher VNU, which also published *Electronic Design*. In 1995, the magazine ceased publication.

It was gone, but not entirely forgotten. In 2005, Intel advertised that it would pay $10,000 for an original copy of the increasingly rare *Electronics* edition containing the Gordon Moore article. A British engineer claimed the reward, saying he'd use the money to help pay for his daughters' weddings. Explaining why he'd kept the magazine and dozens of other issues for all these years, the engineer said: "I thought you shouldn't throw them out because they [were] recording the golden age of electronics."

GREEN BUILDING

Built in 1930, the 35-story building in New York served as McGraw-Hill's world headquarters until 1972. Designed by architect Raymond Hood, the blue-green building is considered a classic example of Art Deco style and was designated a National Historic Landmark in 1989.

16

CARVING A PLACE IN CITY SKYLINES

"The skyscraper problem is new, we have practically no tradition," observed architect Raymond Hood in the 1930s. As a result, he said, architects "are all as free as the wind in trying out every idea that comes into our heads."

One result: The McGraw-Hill Building at 330 West 42nd Street in New York, designed by Hood and built in 1930. It would be "the Middle West Side's most imposing edifice," in the words of one New York City guidebook. Or, in the opinion of another observer, it was a "storm center" that showed "disregard for every accepted principle of architectural designing in the most flagrant manner." (Hood also designed the Tribune Building in Chicago and the strikingly unadorned New York Daily News Building at the opposite end of 42nd St.)

Simply described, the McGraw-Hill building was a 35-story "tiered layer cake" that stood flush to the sidewalk at the bottom, then with two setbacks, each several stories high. At the top, a "heavy ornamental crown" bore the words "McGraw-Hill." Art Deco light fixtures and decorative touches graced the entrance way.

But it was the dramatic coloring that stood out and generated controversy: The first-floor exterior was marked by horizontal strips of olive-green and dark blue terra-cotta tile. Above, the metal window frames contained bits of vermillion, while the window shades were buff-colored.

Modernists approved of what would become known as the Green Building, however. Observed *Architectural Forum*: "No attempt has been made to treat the building as anything other than it is—a series of factory floors, varying in size only to conform to the zoning laws that require setbacks and superimposed to a height dictated by the economics of the project." Most of the building was occupied by McGraw-Hill, with several lower floors devoted to printing presses and a composing department and floors just above, to book bindery and production.

The beyond-10th-Avenue, Hell's Kitchen site was dictated by

city zoning laws, which restricted new factories—including printing plants—to the edges of town. Hood's building loomed over other, more modest neighborhood structures. Still, its inhabitants seemed to like it. Jack Dierdorff, who would in time become *BusinessWeek*'s managing editor, recalled: "Our office was on the west side of the 31st floor, and we could look out the windows and see the ocean liners at the docks. I began getting the steamship news so I could identify which ships they were." In 1989, the building was declared a National Historic Landmark by the U.S. Department of the Interior.

Two previous company buildings had also made a mark on the New York City skyline. In the early part of the 20th century, McGraw Publishing had occupied an 11-story building on 39th Street. In 1914, the Hill Publishing Co. opened its new 12-story, steel-frame-and-plate-glass headquarters at 36th and 10th Avenue. When the McGraw and Hill companies were consolidated in 1917, book operations remained on 39th Street while magazine staff moved into the Hill building

As the years went by, 330 West 42nd Street could not contain all of the growing corporation's New York employees. They were already spread out in six separate buildings. So, in 1967 McGraw-Hill announced that it was beginning construction of a new 50-story headquarters at 1221 Avenue of the Americas and 49th Street. Now, it would be nearer to the rest of Manhattan publishing, right at Rockefeller Center.

The new building would be part of a three-block office-building complex. Other participants included Standard Oil (which would occupy a similar building immediately across 49th St.) and Celanese (47-48th Streets). The three buildings were not uniform, despite architect Wallace Harrison's nickname for them, "the X,Y,Z buildings."

The McGraw-Hill structure included a 110-foot-wide sunken plaza and a 40-foot-by-200-foot park at the rear. For the building's exterior, this time the company went with a simple brown granite that "would wear well" and "not show dirt," in the words of former Chairman Donald C. McGraw. The new structures were, again, not to everyone's taste: the *New York Times* architecture critic Paul Goldberger once excoriated the trio of buildings as "banal in the extreme" but with the passage of time admitted "they do have a certain presence."

New York City is not alone in having a skyline on which McGraw-Hill has left a lasting imprint. The company has

1.

2.

"Our green building initiative is aimed at protecting the environment by helping conserve energy and natural resources."
—Roopa Kudva, CRISIL CEO

long had a presence in London, including financial services and book publishing. In 2004, several hundred employees formerly housed in eight separate locations all moved into a new state-of-the art London headquarters in East London's Canary Wharf financial district. The 20 Canada Square building is home to units of Standard & Poor's, S&P Capital IQ and Platts.

In 2007, Dubuque, Iowa, became home to the company's first fully environmentally sustainable building, housing McGraw-Hill Education's global headquarters for its higher education, science, engineering, and math group. The building received LEED Silver certification by the U.S. Green Building Council in 2008 and set the standard for all of the company's new construction and renovation projects. The building was constructed using regionally manufactured and recycled materials and features preferred parking for hybrid vehicles, a white roof to reduce solar heat absorption and plumbing fixtures that reduce water consumption by 30 percent.

And in 2010, CRISIL—the leading ratings, research, and policy-advisory company in India whose major shareholder is S&P—moved into its new eco-friendly headquarters in Mumbai.

6.

3.

4.

5.

Dubbed "CRISIL House," the building is designed to let in lots of natural light and thereby cut electricity use. It also has a roof garden and "green areas" on alternate floors. "Our green building initiative is aimed at protecting the environment by helping conserve energy and natural resources," said CRISIL CEO Roopa Kudva.

Other major offices of McGraw-Hill include 55 Water St., in the Financial District of Manhattan. The building on the edge of the East River is home to Standard & Poor's, S&P Capital IQ and S&P Dow Jones Indices. Further uptown near Pennsylvania Station and Madison Square Garden sits 2 Penn Plaza, home to McGraw-Hill Construction, including Dodge and *Architectural Record*, Platts, Aviation Week and McGraw-Hill Education.

Just outside New York, the company has a sizable presence in East Windsor, N.J. What began in 1958 as a consolidation has grown over the years into one of McGraw-Hill's largest facilities. The company originally set up there after it decided to move its book shipping business out of New York City in the 1950s. Since then, data processing capabilities, voice and data transmission and other operations have been added at the Hightstown location.

McGraw-Hill's timeless "The Man in the Chair" advertisement first appeared in *BusinessWeek* and *Advertising Age* in May 1958. The original Man was Gil Morris, an ad agency executive.

"I don't know who you are.

I don't know your company.

I don't know your company's product.

I don't know what your company stands for.

I don't know your company's customers.

I don't know your company's record.

I don't know your company's reputation.

Now—what was it you wanted to sell me?"

17

BALDING, BESPECTACLED AND BOW-TIED: AN ICON IS BORN

They're cantankerous and feisty but always memorable—and sometimes even a little lovable. Curmudgeons.

McGraw-Hill has its own curmudgeon—so true-to-life, astute, and adaptable that for many years he has been among the company's most recognized faces. He is "The Man in the Chair"—or, as he was once known, "The I-Don't-Know Man."

"The Man in the Chair" first appeared in 1958, in advertisements that ran in *Advertising Age* and McGraw-Hill publications. His 52-word rant was created by advertising firm Fuller, Smith, and Ross. The Man himself was none other than an agency executive, Gil Morris, who seemed to fit the role perfectly. An impromptu Polaroid shot of Morris that was never intended for formal use went on to become an icon.

Balding, bespectacled, and bow-tied, the Man levels an unforgiving look on the viewer.

"I don't know who you are," he begins. "I don't know your company. I don't know your company's product. I don't know what your company stands for. I don't know your company's customers. I don't know your company's record. I don't know your company's reputation.

Now—what was it you wanted to sell me?"

The moral of this dressing-down is delivered on a tagline at the bottom of the page: "Sales start before your salesman calls—with business publication advertising." In other words, business-to-business advertising pays.

"The Man in the Chair" received lots of advertising industry kudos. In the year of its first appearance, *Advertising Age* selected it as one of the "Ten Best Advertisements of the Year." It was further celebrated in such books as Fred C. Poppe's *100 Greatest Corporate and Industrial Ads* (1997). And in a 1979 report on the top advertisements of all time, *Advertising Age* observed: "Have you ever read an ad that expresses the 'it pays to advertise' philosophy any better?"

"The theme of the ad is timeless. It speaks to the importance of business relationships, customer focus, and value creation."

—Glenn Goldberg, McGraw-Hill's president of Commodities and Commercial Markets

More importantly, the public showed its favor by requesting reprints by the thousands. In the first year, the company received requests for over 100,000 reprints. That number doubled within three years.

The original black-and-white ad was such a success it ran for a decade. In 1968, a full-color version began running, with an even-more-curmudgeonly Arthur Tell taking over the throne. Four years later, a more youthful looking executive with a sporty suit assumed the role.

The advertisement ran in numerous foreign languages, including French, Russian, German, Italian—and Chinese, with a male Chinese curmudgeon, for a monthly magazine distributed in China. In 1991, F.W. Dodge bulletins began using a version featuring a hardhat-wearing construction worker, and in 1996, an Asian woman took over the scolding duties.

The basic message of the ad remains as relevant as ever. That was the theme of a dramatic presentation at the 2009 meeting of the Business Marketing Association, featuring a live reading of the famous rant—and an updated version.

"I didn't find you on Google, your website is totally thin, I looked for you on LinkedIn...and I see an ex-employee out there is doing some pretty nasty blogging about your CEO," the modern presenter intoned. "Now, what was it you wanted to sell me?"

Would McGraw-Hill ever use the ad again?

"The theme of the ad is timeless," said Glenn Goldberg, McGraw-Hill's president of Commodities and Commercial Markets. "It speaks to the importance of business relationships, customer focus, and value creation. It can certainly be adapted to today's web and wireless-enabled world. In fact, it may be even *more* relevant today, when it's easy to mistake the ubiquity of communication devices with quality communication and relationship-building."

"I don't know who you are.
I don't know your company.
I don't know your company's product.
I don't know what your company stands for.
I don't know your company's customers.
I don't know your company's record.
I don't know your company's reputation.
Now—what was it you wanted to sell me?"

MORAL: Sales start **before** your salesman calls—with business publication advertising.

McGRAW-HILL MAGAZINES
BUSINESS • PROFESSIONAL • TECHNICAL

" I don't know who you are.

I don't know your company.

I don't know your company's product.

I don't know what your company stands for.

I don't know your company's customers.

I don't know your company's record.

I don't know your company's reputation.

Now – what was it you wanted to sell me?"

CEO Harold W. McGraw, Jr.
speaks at a news conference
about the hostile takeover
attempt by American Express,
on Jan. 16, 1979.

18

HOLDING TRUE TO VALUES

It's hard to imagine any major enterprise that has been around for as long as McGraw-Hill has succeeding without encountering at least a few challenges.

In McGraw-Hill's case, adversity has always been met head-on by being independent, transparent and honest— values at the core of its business.

These values helped inform McGraw-Hill's response to the 1979 hostile takeover attempt by American Express.

In January of that year, American Express' Chairman James D. Robinson III and President Roger Morley approached CEO Harold W. McGraw, Jr., with a bid to buy the company for $34 a share, or a total of $830 million in cash. That was far higher than the roughly $26 a share the stock was trading at the time.

McGraw was startled by the bid, particularly by the fact that Morley also served as a Director on McGraw-Hill's Board. He believed that Morley had violated his fiduciary duties, misappropriating confidential information.

And by the very next day, McGraw, firmly determined to resist, rallied the Corporate Board to unanimously reject what he termed an "illegal, improper, unsolicited and surprising" takeover proposal.

He drafted a letter of refusal that was published as a mid-January, two-page ad in the *New York Times* and *The Wall Street Journal*.

"We intend to spare absolutely no effort in protecting McGraw-Hill," the letter concluded.

The defense—which also involved legal action including a breach-of-trust lawsuit focused on Morley and a rejection by stockholders—all prompted American Express to withdraw its bid.

Nine years earlier, McGraw also called upon the company's values when dealing with another matter—one author's elaborate hoax.

"There was advice to ignore the whole thing," he said, "but a couple of us said: 'We're built on integrity. You've got to get to the bottom of something, open the thing up, get in the police.'"

Added then McGraw-Hill CEO Shelton Fisher, the company was "determined to 'go all the way' to get at the truth," even though filing charges of fraud and forgery "would whip the unwanted winds of publicity to gale force."

The executives were talking about what became world famous in the 1970s as the Howard Hughes-Clifford Irving hoax—which later went on to become the subject of books and movies.

A Reply to an "Unconscionable" Action

To the Board of Directors
American Express Company:

The McGraw-Hill Board of Directors has unanimously instructed me to **categorically reject your request to discuss the illegal, improper, unsolicited, and surprising American Express proposal to take over McGraw-Hill.**

Further, the McGraw-Hill Board, upon the advice of independent legal counsel, has directed management to **vigorously protect the integrity and vital interests of this company against any takeover attempt you may launch.**

You should understand that there are several significant and fundamental reasons that dictate this determination.

1. The *independence* and *credibility* of McGraw-Hill is vital to fulfilling its responsibilities to investors, the academic, educational, and scientific communities, as well as those who rely on the information and advisory services we offer.

It would be improper, inappropriate, and in direct violation of this responsibility to entrust McGraw-Hill's sensitive public interest activities (including Business Week and the Standard & Poor's credit rating services) to a company that pays virtually no federal income taxes on its hundreds of millions of dollars of annual income, operates in a manner that raises serious questions under the banking and securities laws, and pays no interest on the billions of dollars it derives from the issuance of travelers checks to the public.

One dramatic illustration of the potential for serious conflict of interest is the fact that, as a major investor in securities, American Express holds more than $3 billion in state and municipal securities and underwrites and insures additional state and municipal securities—securities that must be independently rated by McGraw-Hill's Standard & Poor's division!

The background and manner of your proposal demonstrates that American Express lacks the integrity, corporate morality, and sensitivity to professional responsibility essential to the McGraw-Hill publishing, broadcasting, and credit rating services relied upon by so many people.

Frankly, this surprises us. Such insensitivity and disregard of integrity and corporate morality is inconsistent with the reputation many American Express directors have enjoyed over the years. **Perhaps it can be explained as impulsive, precipitous, and immature actions taken by younger members of your management before the more experienced members of your board had ample opportunity to fully consider this reckless proposal and all of its implications to each company.**

Mr. Roger H. Morley, President of American Express, was a director of McGraw-Hill when you formulated and made your proposal. He clearly violated his fiduciary duties to McGraw-Hill and the stockholders of McGraw-Hill by **misappropriating confidential information and conspiring with American Express, the members of the Board of Directors of American Express, and others** to acquire McGraw-Hill at a price, in a manner, and at a time that would be most beneficial to American Express, but **to the detriment of McGraw-Hill's stockholders.**

This breach of trust and conspiracy to subvert the interests of McGraw-Hill and its stockholders was **initiated in the spring of 1978** by your Chairman, Mr. James D. Robinson, III. In seeking to solicit our interest in a merger with American Express, Mr. Robinson gave me his absolute word and assurance that if we were not interested in pursuing the matter, nothing further would be done. **It was not in McGraw-Hill's best interest** and so I made it clear that we were not interested in pursuing it. Yet, as recent events have shown, American Express continued in its plan and preparation. In light of this, **Mr. Morley's remaining on the McGraw-Hill Board of Directors for several months following the rejection of Mr. Robinson's approach and our being assured that it would be dropped was insidious. The obvious conflict of interest created by your secret plan to pursue an acquisition of McGraw-Hill while Mr. Morley remained a director is an unprecedented breach of trust.**

American Express' conspiratorial approach and lack of integrity is further emphasized by your obtaining the financing for acquisition of McGraw-Hill from Morgan Guaranty Trust Company which, for more than 50 years, has been McGraw-Hill's principal bank—a fact well known to your Mr. Morley. **Any company that would use its financial power to cause a bank to violate its relationship with a client lacks the integrity and morality essential to the business of McGraw-Hill.**

"We intend to spare absolutely no effort in protecting McGraw-Hill."
—CEO Harold W. McGraw, Jr. in a letter of refusal

In 1970, writer Clifford Irving told McGraw-Hill that Hughes, the world's richest man, a daring aviator and known recluse, had sent him several letters expressing interest in an authorized biography that Irving would write.

Irving convinced McGraw-Hill, which had published three of Irving's previous seven books, that Hughes had really commissioned him. So the company gave Irving a tentative go-ahead. After being fed a great deal of further back-and-forth over ensuing months—including submission of a forged letter of agreement between Irving and Hughes that was vetted by handwriting experts—the company signed a contract for the book, ultimately paying $700,000 in advances.

Soon, Irving produced a compelling manuscript—based in large measure, it later came out, on an unpublished memoir written by Hughes's longtime right-hand man.

"It's, I suppose, 95% right, because he cribbed the information here, there, and the next place, and the 5% of pure invention is pure genius," said Edward Booher, then president of McGraw-Hill's Book Division.

It didn't take long for the fraud to fall apart. Irving didn't expect Hughes to expose his lies, but that's exactly what happened. Hughes came forward to announce that he'd never met Irving and that the whole story was fake.

In 1972, Irving was ordered to pay back his advance; he, his wife Edith (also known as Helga Hughes—a name she used to deposit some of the advance in a Swiss bank), and a man named Richard Suskind all went to prison.

The events had a positive effect for McGraw-Hill, said Theodore Weber, then a public affairs officer.

"We improved our image with a number of audiences," including authors and the working press, he said. "It certainly made us more vocal about our obligations and our tradition in publishing."

(To read about the company's response to the 2008 U.S. housing market crash and the role of Standard & Poor's, please see Chapter 2.)

McGraw-Hill released this app in 2012 in partnership with the Better Business Bureau's Military Line. The Military & Money App is the first free financial educational app that gives servicemembers and their families tools to reduce debt and maximize savings.

McGraw-Hill

VIDEO
BASIC
TRAINING

FINANCIAL
RESOURCES
TOOLBOX
»

MAKE
ANGE
NOW

TIP OF THE DAY

The Servicemembers Civil Relief Act (SCRA) can give you better interest rates and protections for your credit cards.

19

CORPORATE RESPONSIBILITY: EMPOWER THE PUBLIC, PROTECT THE ENVIRONMENT

McGraw-Hill believes in transparency and understanding for all. And that figures prominently in the company's corporate responsibility programs.

Chief among its goals is advancing financial literacy, an aim that has been sharpened since the mid-1990s. McGraw-Hill partners with community organizations around the world to provide access to financial education by donating money, expertise and products.

"The corporation's philanthropic efforts are part of a larger picture of corporate citizenship," said Louise Raymond, vice president for Corporate Responsibility & Sustainability.

"We look at corporate responsibility through a broad lens, considering the impact of our business on a variety of stakeholders and seeking opportunities for innovation and product development," she said.

The company's financial literacy campaign provides resources to teachers, students, and the general public. It has taught some 205,000 students money skills, trained 2,520 teachers and introduced 7,400 elementary school children to financial basics.

A partnership with the New York Public Library led to the opening of Financial Literacy Central, a resource center dedicated to improving people's personal finance skills. Among other activities, the center offers Financial Planning Day in New York City, an all-day affair that provides people with free counseling on finances, credit and planning for the future.

Other work includes partnering with the Better Business Bureau's Military Line to deliver financial literacy and consumer protection programs to military families. In 2012, the partnership launched a free mobile app designed to help military families make better financial decisions, which can be hampered by their long deployments and frequent moves. The Military & Money App is the first financial educational app targeted to servicemembers and their families. Tools include training videos on budgeting and managing debt, calculators to track cash flow, build savings and cut debt, and regular reminders to save.

Microfinance is another aim of McGraw-Hill's corporate responsibility program. Microfinance has become an increasingly popular tool that helps entrepreneurs by providing them loans from a variety of sources—including everyday people who give as little as $5 at a time. McGraw-Hill's grant-making supports

"We look at corporate responsibility through a broad lens, considering the impact of our business on a variety of stakeholders and seeking opportunities for innovation and product development."
—Louise Raymond, Vice President for Corporate Responsibility & Sustainability

microfinance institutions such as the Microfinance Information Exchange and its project to facilitate better reporting of financial and social data by other microfinance institutions.

In partnership with Pro Mujer, a women's development and microfinance organization, McGraw-Hill funded a project to standardize fundamentals of financial skills training so they

1.

2.

3.

4. McGraw-Hill and The New York Public Library opened Financial Literacy Central, an information hub in Manhattan dedicated to helping New Yorkers improve their personal finances in 2010. **5.** CEO Harold McGraw III and Leo O'Neill, President of Standard & Poor's, present a contribution to the company of Engine 4, Ladder 15, of the New York Fire Department on October 11, 2001. The contribution to the unit's Family Fund was made in memory of members who lost their lives in the World Trade Center attack on Septmber 11, 2001. **6.** McGraw and New York City Mayor Michael Bloomberg announce a McGraw-Hill sponsored program to promote reading by waiving late fees for overdue library books in 2011.

could be easily adapted to the many cultures in Argentina, Bolivia, Mexico, Nicaragua and Peru. The program reaches more than a quarter-million women.

McGraw-Hill has also made investments in programs critical to the stability and quality of life in New York City, its global headquarters. Longtime beneficiaries include social-and-community-services center Hartley House and many of the city's arts and cultural institutions, including the classical-music radio program Young Artists Showcase.

Thanks to the company's employee gift-matching program, millions of dollars have gone to support causes ranging from health care to disaster relief. In 2011 the company contributed nearly $2 million through its matching programs to causes including disaster relief for the tsunami in Japan and the famine in East Africa.

Company employees regularly donate their time to communities as part of the corporation's annual Global Volunteer Day. More than 6,000 employees donated some 40,000 hours on 280 community projects in 19 countries through the company's volunteering programs in 2011.

The McGraw-Hill Research Foundation, another major focus of the company, partners with academic, business, and nonprofit organizations to advance education and knowledge, and raise social awareness about key societal issues and trends that contribute to global growth and prosperity by publishing papers by thought leaders and holding events.

"In a short period of time, The McGraw-Hill Research Foundation has become a respected advocate for advancing knowledge in the 21st century," said research foundation President James H. McGraw IV. "Through research, the papers we publish, and events we sponsor, we're drawing attention to important issues and advancing necessary changes."

CEO Harold McGraw III and Chairman Emeritus Harold W. McGraw, Jr., with the 2008 winners of the Harold W. McGraw, Jr. Prize in Education. From back left: Project Lead The Way Vice President Richard Blais, Judth Berry Griffin, founder of The Ophelia J. Berry Fund and Dr. Charles B. Reed, California State University System Chancellor.

Kathleen Ross was taken aback when her friends suggested starting their own college. She understood that the recently announced closure of Ft. Wright College, where she was academic vice president, meant an end to college opportunities for students living in the Yakima Nation Indian Reservation in Washington State. Hesitantly, she decided to follow her friends' suggestion and help form a new institution, to be known as Heritage College. It officially opened in 1982 in a former elementary school building in Toppenish, Washington. Total student population: 85. More than half of the students were either Native American or Hispanic; the average age was 35. Ross became Heritage College's first president.

In 1989, Ross became one of the first winners of the Harold W. McGraw, Jr. Prize in Education. "Armed only with a vision, she brought higher education to a population living largely below the poverty level," read the Prize announcement. The college continues to succeed. Now known as Heritage University, by 2011 it had more than 1,200 students and offered both undergraduate and graduate degrees.

The Harold W. McGraw, Jr. Prize in Education dates from 1988, when it was begun as part of the company's 100th anniversary celebration. The Prize is named

President George H.W. Bush honors Harold W. McGraw, Jr. in 1990 with a National Literacy Honors medal.

after the former CEO, who had a lifelong commitment to learning.

From the Prize's beginning, an independent board has selected three annual winners whose programs and ideas can serve as effective models for others. Each receives an award of $50,000 and a bronze statuette. The awards are presented at a black-tie dinner, where each winner also speaks about his or her experience.

Since the Prize's inception, awardees have ranged from distinguished professors of education to public school teachers and principals, from state governors to school-system superintendents. Frequently, educators who have sought to address the problems of underserved communities and the underprivileged have been recipients. Among these have been Ross; Helen "Jinx" Crouch, president of the Literacy Volunteers of America; Geoffrey Canada, creator of the Harlem Children's Zone, which seeks to encourage a culture of education in that community; and Wendy Kopp, president and founder of Teach for America, which enlists recent college grads to commit to two years of teaching in under-resourced urban and rural areas.

Another highly deserving winner was Columbia University psychology professor Kenneth B. Clark, whose research into the damaging effect of separate-but-equal education played a key role in the landmark 1954 Supreme Court decision in *Brown v. Board of Education*, which outlawed school segregation.

By the late 2000s, Prizes have been given for innovators who are weaving technology into education. Sal Khan, executive director and founder of the Khan Academy, won in 2012 for his nonprofit's mission of providing free, high-quality education for "anyone, anywhere" in the world through thousands of videos on a myriad of topics posted on YouTube.

Harold W. McGraw, Jr. was steadfast in his devotion to education. In addition to his leadership of McGraw-Hill, he founded a national organization to combat illiteracy, the Business Council for Effective Literacy, personally providing it with $1 million in startup funding. He was honored in 1990, when President George H.W. Bush presented him with a National Literacy Honors medal. "Your grandfather, James McGraw, began as a teacher before turning to publishing," Bush said. "It now seems so very appropriate that you should turn from publishing to a very special type of teaching—teaching your business colleagues."

In presenting the 2012 Prize in Education winners, CEO Harold McGraw III pledged to continue the Prize with McGraw Hill Financial.

"As we celebrate 25 years of educational achievement and mark the next chapter in our business, I am privileged to pledge to you our ongoing commitment to this Prize—to its legacy, to my father, and to all the winners who have distinguished the Prize and who have built its reputation."

James H. McGraw meets with President Herbert Hoover at the White House in the fall of 1929 at the National Conference of Business Paper Editors.

20

ALWAYS DEDICATED TO BUSINESS LEADERSHIP AT McGRAW-HILL

Through 125 years of growth, innovation and transformation, McGraw-Hill has been guided by the steady hands of leaders who instilled in the company the same principles it was founded on: editorial independence, truth and remarkably high standards.

The company's story begins with James H. McGraw, a former schoolteacher from the village of Panama in western New York State who joined the staff of The American Railway Publishing Co. in 1884 as a salesman, enamored by the radical innovation of the 1800s—the railroad.

After only a year, McGraw learned that his employer was in financial straits. Borrowing $1,000 from an old friend, and using $1,500 he was owed in commissions, he invested in the company and became a vice-president. Then in 1888 McGraw left with full control of a prize property, *The American Journal of Railway Appliances*. It would become the acorn from which two global powerhouses—one focused on financial intelligence, the other on education, would grow.

Soon, *The Street Railway Journal*, devoted to the electrification of street railways across the U.S., became McGraw's premier

1.

publication. Other early journals included *Electrical World and Engineer*, and *American Electrician*, both dedicated to keeping up with the rapid pace of industrial progress in America

In 1899, with the intention of adding more publications to his stable, McGraw established the McGraw Publishing Co. He would later publish *Electrochemical Industry*, *Engineering Record*, and *The Plumber and Sanitary Engineer*.

It seemed to make sense to package some of these journals' practical articles in book form—leading to the 1907 publication of the *Standard Handbook for Electrical Engineers*. And within two years, McGraw had linked his book-publishing operation to that of the similarly inclined John Hill, forming the McGraw-Hill

2.

3.

Book Co. The book company's first catalog listed 200 titles, including one by a future U.S. president, Herbert Hoover's *Principles of Mining*. Over the next 20 years, McGraw-Hill became an extensive publisher of scientific and economic books, expanding its list of titles to more than 1,600.

In 1917, after Hill's death, all McGraw and Hill operations were merged with the formation of the McGraw-Hill Publishing Co. Inc., under the president James H. McGraw. The company founder laid down strict rules for editorial integrity. "For while the business of publishing is a commercial enterprise, at its core it is professional. If the commercial should dominate, the enterprise would lose in public confidence," he wrote.

In the 1920s, James H. McGraw became less active, and his four sons—James Jr., Curtis, Harold, and Donald—took over management of the company. On February 14, 1929, the company went public with a listing on the New York Stock Exchange.

In looking back at the enterprise he had built, McGraw said the company's success in books and business publications was a result of being founded on sound principles of service. He offered that to maintain the public's confidence, the business press must always conduct itself "with an eye single to the interests of the reader." In 1935, James H. McGraw, Jr. became president and chairman, succeeded in 1950 by Curtis W. McGraw. Three years later, Donald C. McGraw became president. Under their leadership, the company established McGraw-Hill World News Service, acquired the forerunner to commodities information provider Platts and published seminal textbooks such as Paul Sameulson's *Economics*.

4. Harold W. McGraw, Sr. with the McGraw-Hill baseball team.
5. Harold McGraw, Jr. in 1963. He joined McGraw-Hill as a sales representative in 1947 and became executive vice president of the Book Co. in 1965 and its president in 1968. He became CEO in 1975.

4.

5.

The McGraws spent time learning the business when they joined the company. Donald C. McGraw, for example, who would later become chairman of McGraw-Hill in 1953, entered the company in 1919 working for $65 per month (about $525 in 2012 adjusted for inflation).

After some time spent as an assistant to the manager at *Chemical Week*, Donald became interested in the real nuts and bolts of publishing, so he went to the print shop to learn that end of the business. Stints as a pressman and in the composing room preceded years of work in corporate purchasing.

James A. McGraw, a nephew of the company founder, entered McGraw-Hill in the early 1900s as an office boy, then worked in the makeup department of *Architectural Record* before becoming part of advertising sales.

Into the 1960s, McGraw-Hill was an increasingly prosperous company consisting of three divisions— magazines, books, and the newly acquired F.W. Dodge, which focused on providing insights and intelligence in the booming construction industry. There were 7,200 employees in 1962 and revenue was about $100 million.

Shelton Fisher became president in 1966 and took over the role of chief executive officer from Donald in 1968. Fisher served as CEO until 1975. During Fisher's tenure, the company acquired Standard & Poor's, television stations and moved McGraw-Hill's headquarters to a brand new building in Rockefeller Center in Manhattan.

Harold W. McGraw, Jr. would become president of the corporation in 1974 and CEO the following year. He joined the company in 1947 as a sales representative with

1.

2.

the Book Co., becoming president of that unit in 1968. Harold's heart remained firmly anchored in book publishing. During a 1956 Columbia University oral history interview, he expounded at length on book-publishing achievements, particularly noting several successful titles: *Betty Crocker's Picture Cook Book*; a series of best-selling, religion-themed books by Catherine Marshall (including *A Man Called Peter*); and the memoirs of General Douglas MacArthur. Such popular volumes propelled McGraw-Hill books to double its 1950s sales, to $84.4 million by 1965—more than one-third of the $216.2 million in revenue the company made that year. By 1980, revenues had passed $1 billion.

Under Harold W. McGraw, Jr.'s leadership, McGraw-Hill successfully fended off an unwanted attempt by American Express to take over the company in 1979. (To read more on the takeover attempt, see Chapter 18.)

Harold always believed that the quality and content of the message, rather than the mode of delivery, were most important. "Although the medium might change," he said, "content always must be determined by the same standards—it has to be accurate, objective, authoritative, comprehensive, current, and reliable."

Those principles served the company well, as they have throughout time. Under Harold's eight years as CEO, the company's revenue more than doubled and earnings per share more than tripled.

Harold retired in 1983 and became chairman emeritus in 1988, remaining an active presence within the corporation.

With McGraw's retirement, Joseph L. Dionne, a longtime executive with the company became CEO. During his tenure, Dionne built up McGraw-Hill Education by, among other things, entering into a joint venture with Macmillan, the textbook publisher that was a unit of Maxwell Communication Corp. He also pushed the company's employees to leverage the wealth of information that existed in McGraw-Hill's printed products into new electronic platforms. He embraced technology and as he once told the *New York Times*, the "computer could be used not only to create new products, but also to enhance existing ones, and that

3.

4.

"At the company's very beginning, one magazine was all about helping readers understand and benefit from the changing landscape of the time. That focus does not change."
—CEO Harold McGraw III

no matter what equipment people use, McGraw-Hill should provide them with the information pertinent to their business. Whatever form our information products take, when we offer something, it has to be the very best."

McGraw-Hill's Board of Directors appointed Harold McGraw III as CEO in 1998 to succeed Dionne, and the following year the Board elected McGraw chairman. McGraw (known as Terry) joined the company in 1980 as vice president of Corporate Planning, and went on to serve as publisher of *Aviation Week & Space Technology*, president of the McGraw-Hill Publications Co., and president of the McGraw-Hill Financial Services Company. He became president and COO in 1993. In 1979, McGraw left his job in corporate finance at GTE to join forces with his father, to successfully fight the hostile takeover attempt by American Express. "I realized that this company was special, and I really wanted to work here," he recalled years later. "After about seven or eight months I quit my job and joined McGraw-Hill full time."

Under McGraw's stewardship, McGraw-Hill expanded into new markets while keeping a sharp focus on client needs and advancing shareholder value.

Upon becoming president, McGraw set out to transform the company from a fragmented collection of financial and information businesses

into a more focused group. He reduced the company's dependency on cyclical advertising-based businesses and concentrated on higher-growth digital businesses. In 2011, McGraw-Hill sold its Broadcasting Group, a collection of ABC affiliates and Azteca America TV stations, and divested *BusinessWeek* to Bloomberg L.P. in 2009. Earlier he sold publications like *Chemical Engineering.*

He focused on increasing the company's subscription-based businesses, such as Platts. (See Chapter 5 for more.) He invested in organic growth and strategic partnerships, such as the joint venture S&P Dow Jones Indices. And he built size and scale in the financial data, research and analytics business, S&P Capital IQ. This business has

grown its client base from 1,000 in mid-2005 to more than 3,800 at the end of 2011, a 21% compound annual growth rate. (See Chapter 3 for more.)

Between 1993, when McGraw became president, and 2012, McGraw-Hill returned more than $13 billion to shareholders in the form of dividends and share repurchases. And the company's stock increased more than six-fold, from $8.20 a share to $54.67, through the end of 2012.

There's great continuity in McGraw-Hill's mission, McGraw reflects. "At the company's very beginning, one magazine was all about helping readers understand and benefit from the changing landscape of the time. That focus does not change."

On Left: CEO Harold McGraw III at the New York Stock Exchange in 2011. **Above:** James H. McGraw received an honorary degree in Commercial Science in 1929 from New York University for being a "publisher who has never ceased to be an educator."

McGRAW-HILL BOARD OF DIRECTORS IN 2012

Front row from left:

Sir Winfried Bischoff
Chairman of Lloyds Banking Group plc

Edward B. Rust, Jr.
Presiding Director of the McGraw-Hill Board, Chairman and Chief Executive Officer of State Farm Insurance Companies

Harold McGraw III
Board Chairman, President and Chief Executive Officer of McGraw-Hill

Linda Koch Lorimer
Vice President and Secretary of Yale University

Sidney Taurel
Chairman Emeritus, Eli Lilly and Company

Back row from left:

Robert P. McGraw
Chairman and Chief Executive Officer of Averdale Holdings LLC

Hilda Ochoa-Brillembourg
Founder, President and Chief Executive Officer of Strategic Investment Group

William D. Green
Chairman of Accenture

Charles E. "Ed" Haldeman, Jr.
Former Chief Executive Officer of Freddie Mac

Sir Michael Rake
Chairman of BT Group plc

Pedro Aspe
Co-Chairman of Evercore Partners, Inc.

Kurt L. Schmoke
Dean, Howard University School of Law

Richard E. Thornburgh
Vice Chairman, Corsair Capital LLC

McGRAW-HILL LEADERSHIP IN 2012

Principal Corporate Executives

Harold McGraw III
Chairman, President and Chief Executive Officer

Jack F. Callahan, Jr.
Executive Vice President
and Chief Financial Officer

John L. Berisford
Executive Vice President, Human Resources

D. Edward Smyth
Executive Vice President, Corporate Affairs and
Executive Assistant to the Chairman, President
and Chief Executive Officer

Charles L. Teschner, Jr.
Executive Vice President, Global Strategy

Kenneth M. Vittor
Executive Vice President and General Counsel

Principal Operations Executives

Douglas L. Peterson
President, Standard & Poor's

Louis V. Eccleston
President, S&P Capital IQ and Chairman of the
Board of S&P Dow Jones Indices

Glenn S. Goldberg
President, Commodities and Commercial Markets

Lloyd G. "Buzz" Waterhouse
President and Chief Executive Officer,
McGraw-Hill Education

ACKNOWLEDGMENTS

Mimi Barker

David Blitzer

Sandi Brady

Christopher Chew

Joanna O. dela Rosa

David Dell'Accio

Jeff Dunsavage

Ed Emmer

Jason Feuchtwanger

Emily Fredrix Goodman

Eileen Gabrielle

Hardy Green

Jim Holtje

Jonathan Horn

Celeste Hughes

Marianne Johnston

Jackie Kilberg

Ashley Lau

Tom Lau

Joanne Lee

Catherine Mathis

Peter McCurdy

Chip Merritt

Judy Moseley

Ty Nowicki

John Piecuch

Michael Privitera

Patti Rockenwagner

Don Rubin

Dan Sieger

Ted Smyth

Tom Stanton

John Tews

Kenneth Vittor

Patti Walsh

PHOTO CREDITS

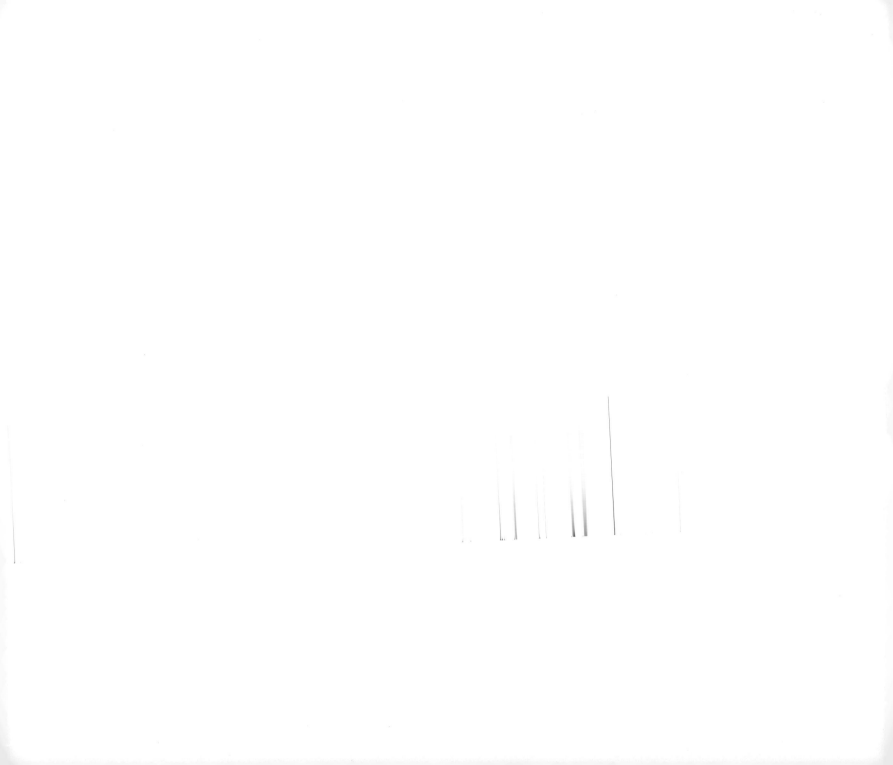